KNIT BABY

Head & Toes!

KNIT BABY

Head & Toes!

Edited by

GWEN STEEGE

Storey Publishing

*The mission of Storey Publishing is to serve our customers by publishing practical
information that encourages personal independence in harmony with the environment.*

Edited by Gwen Steege, Masha Zager, and Karen Levy
Art direction, cover and text design by Susi Oberhelman
Cover photograph by Ross Whitaker
Interior photographs by Zeva Oelbaum
Illustrations by Alison Kolesar
Text production by Jennifer Jepson Smith
Indexed by Susan Olason, Indexes & Knowledge Maps

The information in this book is true and complete to the best of our knowledge. All recommendations
are made without guarantee on the part of the editor or Storey Publishing. The editor and publisher disclaim
any liability in connection with the use of this information. For additional information, please contact Storey
Publishing, 210 MASS MoCA Way, North Adams, MA 01247.

Storey books are available for special premium and promotional uses and for customized editions. For
further information, please call 1-800-793-9396.

Printed in Hong Kong by Elegance Printing

10 9 8 7 6 5 4 3 2 1

Library of Congress Cataloging-in-Publication Data

Knit baby : head & toes! / edited by Gwen Steege.
    p. cm.
ISBN 1-58017-494-4 (alk. paper)
1. Knitting—Patterns. 2. Infants' clothing. I. Title: Head & toes!. II. Steege, Gwen, 1940–

TT825.K623 2003
746.43'20432-dc21

2003041640

Contents

Head-to-Toe Knitting

Knitting for babies is a blast. You can put the most adorable and outrageous things on babies and, providing it is not too itchy, too tight, or too difficult to put on — what do they know? Let's face it, babies are cute in just about anything. If the baby belongs to you or someone you love, he or she will look great in whatever you knit. After all, you made it, stitch by stitch, love looped in quiet moments between the bank and the bus, supper and stories, rinse and spin, the staff meeting, the sidelines, waiting rooms, and gridlock. Small catches of time yielding a piece of art treasured by the maker, the parents, and (in about 20 years) the recipient.

Because these projects are small, ranging in size from newly arrived to the ripe old age of 12 months, you may feel brave enough to take on a more difficult pattern than you've previously dared to. The time and yarn investment is smaller, the knowledge gained greater. You can even use the yarn stash you have on hand; better yet, buy some of the good stuff — it won't take much.

Whether you are new to knitting or have been working those sticks since you were old enough to hold them, the wide range of patterns in *Knit Baby — Head & Toes!* will offer you an opportunity to experiment with many yarns and techniques. The varying skill levels are intended to engage, not enrage. And should you find yourself approaching the hair-pulling, teeth-gnashing stage at any point, it's time to tell yourself to step away from the knit-ting, for this hobby of ours isn't all about result — the process itself is meant to be fun and relaxing.

Above all, remember that babies are such a wonderful gift — it's our pleasure to outfit them in only the best!

The Choice Is Yours

One of the best things about knitting these days is the wonderful variety of colors, textures, and weights of yarns that easily lure you into yarn shops. When you're deciding what kind of yarn to choose — washable wool, cotton, synthetic, and various blends — consider what will feel best on a baby. Will this hat be worn by a newborn and need to be super soft, or does it need to be thick and warm and fit over the ears? Many knitters prefer natural fibers for their hand knits. Even when wet, wool, for instance, is considered warmer than cotton or acrylic, but some babies find wool itchy, or they may be allergic to it. Many wool yarns designed for baby projects are wash-able (also called *superwash*). They are softer and easier to care for, and washability is obviously a plus, since baby clothes require frequent launder-ing. Be sure to follow the washer and dryer temperature and setting advice printed on the yarn label. Note that if you are making a felted knitting project, you can't use washable wool — it won't shrink.

If you use more than one type of yarn in the same project, choose yarns of the same weight.

Then, before beginning, sample each of the yarns when you test the gauge. Different yarns have different degrees of elasticity, or they may differ in the way they knit up, hold their shape, and wash. Always launder a mixed-yarn item according to the directions for the most delicate yarn used. For example, if one yarn is machine washable and another yarn requires hand washing, then the knitted garment made with a combination of these yarns should be hand washed. Be sure to include washing instructions with garments you give as gifts.

A final word about yarns: Very inexpensive yarns stretch easily and pill and, in general, don't hold up well. Knitting is a fun hobby, but when you're putting time and effort into a project, you'll want it to last.

Here are some common yarn sizes, with an estimate of the number of stitches per inch you can expect to get on the needle sizes given.

Baby or fingering yarn
6.5 to 8 stitches = 1 inch   US 0–3

Sport weight yarn
5.5 to 6 stitches = 1 inch   US 4–6

Double knit (DK) yarn
5 to 6 stitches = 1 inch   US 4–6

Worsted weight yarn
4 to 5 stitches = 1 inch   US 6–9

Bulky weight yarn
2 to 3.5 stitches = 1 inch   US 9–11

Don't Be an Itch!

Babies have sensitive skin. If you want to knit something warm but are afraid it will be uncomfortable against delicate skin, choose a hat style with a wide hem, and knit this hem of a fiber other than wool — cotton or silk, for instance.

Yarns come in both circular skeins that must be wound into balls before use and in pull-out skeins that don't need rewinding; for a smoother feed, take the yarn from the inside of these skeins.

If you're substituting a yarn for one recommended in a pattern, make sure you buy the correct amount of yardage. For instance, if a pattern calls for one skein of a 190-yard skein and you're using a yarn packaged in 100-yard skeins, buy two skeins of the substitute yarn. You can usually find this information on the label, or ask at the yarn shop. It's always best to buy an extra skein or two to avoid running short. If you have to return for more yarn, you may find that the shop is either out of it or it is from a different dye lot, which means the colors may be slightly but noticeably different. Some shops will set aside an additional skein for up to a month; most shops also accept unused skeins for cash or credit.

Needle Knowledge

Most knitters have strong preferences when it comes to selecting knitting needles, and the wide variety of choices can be confusing until you try them. Coated aluminum needles are durable but sometimes heavy in larger sizes. Plastic or similar materials are lighter, though they can bend or break. Bamboo needles have become increasingly popular: Yarn moves smoothly along bamboo needles, even in hot, sticky weather, and they're comfortable and quiet to use.

Available in several lengths, straight needles are easy to work with. Some people find shorter needles easier to manage. For projects that have many stitches and don't fit easily onto straight needles, use circular needles. You'll also need circular or double-point needles to knit the cylindrical shapes of most hats and booties. Most of the projects in this book are knit in the round on circular or double-point needles. Circular needles come in different lengths and have a flexible nylon or plastic center.

Double-point needles are used for knitting in the round. You may need to switch from circular to double-point needles when you're decreasing a hat to make the top of the crown, and the stitches on the circular needle stretch too far apart. When possible, choose a set of double-point needles with five to a package. Some patterns require five needles, but even if not, it's always good to have the extra needle in case you lose one.

You also need a set of crochet hooks for picking up dropped stitches, weaving in ends, and finishing some edges.

Knitting needles come in numbered sizes, but it's important to note whether the size is US, UK, or metric — they're all different! You'll quickly notice that in the US system, 0 is very small; in the UK system, 0 is large. This book provides US and metric sizes in all the instructions. To convert to the UK system, follow the chart:

US	Metric	UK
0	2mm	14
1	2.25mm	13
	2.5mm	
2	2.75mm	12
	3mm	11
3	3.25mm	10
4	3.5mm	
5	3.75mm	9
6	4mm	8
7	4.5mm	7
8	5mm	6
9	5.5mm	5
10	6mm	4
10½	6.5mm	3
	7mm	2
	7.5mm	1
11	8mm	0
13	9mm	00
15	10mm	000

Knit to Fit

Babies come in all shapes and sizes. The following charts are intended to give you a general idea of babies' head and feet sizes. When planning your project, think about how old the baby will be when the year rolls around to the time he or she will need it. For instance, it wouldn't be practical to make a warm, felted wool hat with earflaps in an infant size for a baby who will be born in April. She will be able to wear it only a few times before the weather gets too warm. For a baby born in April, knit at least a 6-month size, so she will have something toasty to wear when the weather turns cool along about October.

GIRLS		
Age in Months	Head Circumference	Foot Length
0–3	14–15¾"	3½" (9cm)
3–6	15¾–16¾"	4" (10cm)
6–9	16¾–17¼"	4½" (11cm)
9–12	17¼–17¾"	5" (12cm)

BOYS		
Age in Months	Head Circumference	Foot Length
0–3	14–16¼"	3½" (9cm)
3–6	16¼–17¼"	4" (10cm)
6–9	17¼–17¾"	4½" (11cm)
9–12	17¾–18¼″	5" (12cm)

Speaking Knit

To make instructions more concise, most knitters use abbreviations. If you're new to knitting, they can seem like a foreign language. You may encounter these:

cc	contrasting color
cm	centimeter
cont	continue
dec	decrease/decreasing
dp	double point
inc	increase/increasing
K	knit
K2tog	knit 2 stitches together
M1	make 1
mc	main color
mm	millimeter
P	purl
P2tog	purl 2 stitches together
ppso	pass previous stitch over
psso	pass slip stitch over
p2sso	pass 2 slip stitches over
pu	pick up
rnd(s)	round(s)
sl	slip
ssk	slip, slip, knit the 2 slipped stitches together
st(s)	stitch(es)
St st	stockinette stitch
W&T	wrap and turn
yd(s)	yard(s)

Gauge

Many knitters are so excited to get started on a project that they jump right in, never knitting a test swatch to check the gauge. To avoid frustration (and ripping out your knitting later and starting again), *knit a test swatch.* Every knitter holds the yarn with different tension, and you may have to adjust your needle size up or down to achieve the gauge noted in the pattern.

Here's how it works: If you know that 5 stitches and 7 rows equals 1 inch in a certain yarn with a certain size needle, you can make anything — and it fits. Always calculate your gauge over 4 inches (10cm). That's because counting stitches over 1 inch (2.5cm) can be misleading if your stitches are uneven or if the recommended stitches per inch contains a fraction. Here's an example of how to knit a swatch and figure out gauge:

1. Say a pattern lists the gauge as 16 stitches = 4 inches on size 7 needles. Use size 7 needles to cast on 20 stitches (this is the number of gauge stitches, plus a few extra so that you don't need to measure the edge stitches, which may be uneven).

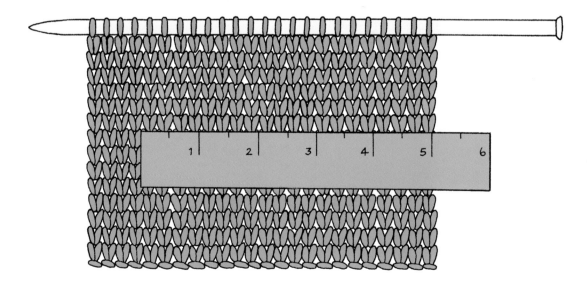

Measuring gauge (16 stitches = 4 inches)

2. Following the stitch pattern you'll be using for the main part of your project (unless the pattern indicates otherwise), knit a swatch about 5 inches long. Do not block the swatch.

3. Lay the swatch on a firm, flat surface. Take care not to stretch the swatch, and make sure the side edges are uncurled. Lay a flat ruler from one side of the swatch to the other. Count the number of stitches within 4 inches (10cm). There should be exactly 16.

4. **If your swatch contains more** than 16 stitches in 4 inches, use larger needles and knit another swatch. Repeat steps 1 through 3.

   If your swatch contains fewer than 16 stitches in 4 inches, use smaller needles and knit another swatch. Repeat steps 1 through 3.

5. Even after you have established what needle size and yarn will get you to the right gauge, after you have knitted a few inches into the project, check again to make sure the gauge is holding true.

NOTE: Always use fresh yarn to make a swatch. Used yarn may be stretched and thus give an inaccurate measurement.

Two needle sizes are sometimes specified for a pattern, the larger for the main body of the hat, and the smaller for ribbing, for instance. If you change your larger-size needles to obtain the correct stitch gauge, adjust the size of the smaller needles to correspond.

Safety First

Here are some important safety issues when making baby garments.

- Don't knit hats (or other items, for that matter) with long tassels or drawstrings that can get wrapped around a baby's neck.
- Small items, such as buttons and beads, can come off a garment and pose a choking hazard. If you do use sewn-on decorative items, make sure they are secured tightly with button thread and cannot be pulled off or loosen over time. Check the items every time the garment is washed.
- Securely weave all yarn ends into the back of the knitted fabric. Yarn ends and long floats can become twisted around small wrists, fingers, and toes, cutting off circulation.

Care Instructions for Baby Gifts

When you give a knitted baby item as a gift, include care instructions. In addition to how to launder the item, remind parents to make sure the garment is free of all soap, as soap residue can irritate a baby's skin and mat the yarn's fibers. Stains can be removed by soaking the garment in cold water while the stain is still wet or by using a commercial stain remover.

Casting On

Casting on with a long-tail cast on makes a neat, firm, but elastic edge for a hat or bootie cuff. If you tend to cast on tightly, you may want to switch to one needle size larger for this part.

1. Estimate how long to make the "tail" by wrapping the yarn around the needle one time for each cast-on stitch you need, then adding a few extra inches. Make a slip knot right here, and slide the knot over a single knitting needle. Hold that needle in your right hand; hold the tail and the working end of the yarn in your left hand. Insert needle through front loop of working yarn loop on your thumb. Wrap tail from back to front around needle.

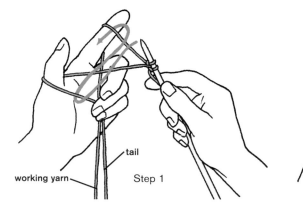

working yarn — tail

Step 1

2. Use the needle to draw the tail through the loop on your thumb.

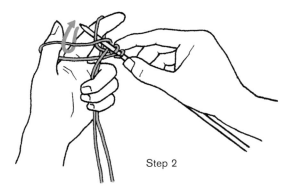

Step 2

3. Release the loop on your thumb, place your thumb underneath the working thread, and draw both toward you while holding the working thread and tail firmly in your fingers.

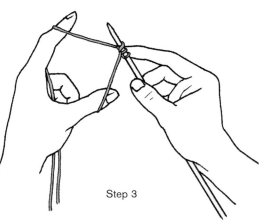

Step 3

Casting Off

Casting off, or binding off, is usually done as follows: Knit two stitches to the right-hand needle, then draw the first one over the second. Don't pull too hard, and use a larger size needle if you knit tightly. Work across the row until one stitch remains, then pull the working end through the last stitch and weave it into the inside.

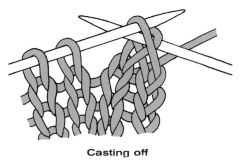

Casting off

THREE-NEEDLE CAST OFF

This is a useful technique if you want to cast off and at the same time join two pieces in an invisible seam. Place half the stitches on one needle and half on a second needle. If you are using straight, single-pointed needles, make sure the needles are pointing in the same direction. Bring the two pieces, or two halves, together with the right sides facing. With a third needle, beginning at the outer edge:

1. Insert the needle through the first stitch on the front and back needles and knit them together.
2. Make a second stitch in the same way.
3. Pass the first stitch over the second one.

Stocking Up

Depending on the project you are knitting, you don't need to purchase all of these items at once. But a well-supplied knitting bag, like all toolkits, makes life easier in many ways.

- Sets of needles, including straight, double-point, and circular
- Set of crochet hooks
- A 6-inch metal ruler with a needle gauge
- Retractable tape measure
- Needle point covers
- Assortment of blunt-pointed tapestry needles
- Box of T-shaped pins
- Small, sharp scissors
- Stitch holders
- Stitch markers, both round and split
- Nice knitting bag

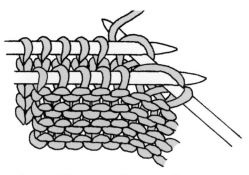

Step 1: Three-needle cast off

Don't Panic!

Beginning knitters often panic when they drop a stitch. It's empowering to discover how easy it is to pick up dropped or half-made stitches. And this is why you need to include a crochet hook in your knitting bag! Working on the right side of stockinette stitch, find the last loop that's still knitted and insert the crochet hook from front to back. (On the wrong side, insert the needle from back to front.) Pull the loop just above the bar between the adjacent stitches, catch the bar with your hook, and draw it through the loop. When picking up a number of stitches, take care to pick up the bars in the correct order.

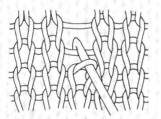

Picking up a dropped stitch knitwise

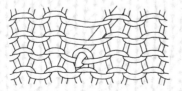

Picking up a dropped stitch purlwise

Increasing

Increases allow you to shape your knitting as you work. Sometimes you'll want these increases to be invisible, but in other cases the increase stitches are not only noticeable but important design elements. It's helpful to learn a variety of techniques so that you can pick and choose whatever is appropriate for your needs. The illustrations that follow show three increase methods: bar increase, make 1 with a right slant, and make 1 with a left slant.

BAR INCREASE

The bar increase (inc) is a tight increase that leaves no hole but shows as a short, horizontal bar on the right side of the fabric. Make it by knitting into the front of the loop in the usual way, but do not remove the stitch from the needle. Instead, knit into the back of the same stitch, and then slip both new stitches onto the right needle.

To increase by two stitches, work into the front loop, the back loop, and the front loop again before taking the three new stitches off the needle.

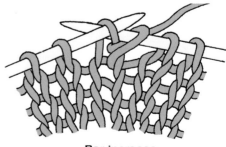

Bar increase

MAKE 1, RIGHT SLANT

1. Look for the horizontal bar between the first stitch on your left-hand needle and the last stitch on your right-hand needle. With the tip of your left needle, pick up this bar from back to front.

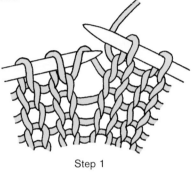

Step 1

2. Knit into the bar from the front, which twists the new stitch and gives it a slant to the right. Even though it may seem a bit difficult to get your needle into the bar from front to back, it's important to do so in order to avoid creating a small hole in the fabric.

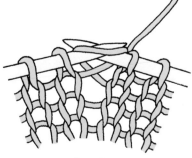

Step 2

MAKE 1, LEFT SLANT

1. Pick up the bar from front to back.

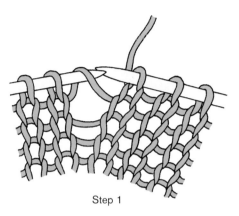

Step 1

2. Knit into the back of the bar, which twists the new stitch to the left.

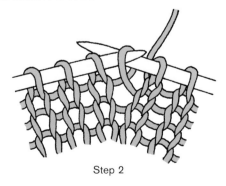

Step 2

NOTE: To make 1 at the end of a round when knitting in the round, pick up the horizontal strand between the first and the last stitches of the round.

Decreasing

As with increasing, decreasing can become an interesting design element in your project, and the pattern directions will specify which method to use. There are three common techniques. Because the first two (ssk and psso) result in a finished stitch that slants to the left, they are often used at the right side of a garment; the last method (K2 tog) results in a right-slanting stitch and so is used on the left edge.

SSK

"Ssk" (slip, slip, knit the two slipped stitches together) is done as follows: Slip two stitches, one at a time, from your left needle to your right, as if to knit. Then, slide the left needle from left to right through the front loops of the slipped stitches, and knit the two stitches together from this position. This technique makes a finished stitch that slants to the left on the finished side and is often used at the beginning of a row.

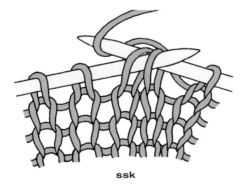

ssk

PSSO

To "psso" (pass slip stitch over knit stitch) in a knit row, slip one stitch from the left needle to the right needle, inserting the needle as if to knit the stitch, but without knitting it. Knit the next stitch, then use the left needle to draw the slipped stitch over the just-knitted stitch. This makes a finished stitch that slants left on the finished side and is another method used at the beginning of a row.

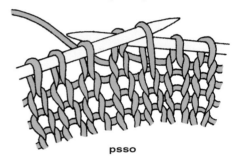

psso

K2TOG

K2tog (knit two stitches together) involves simply inserting the needle into both loops, just as you would to knit. The finished stitch slants to the right on the finished side and is generally used at the end of a row.

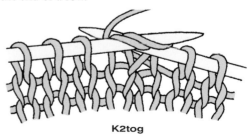

K2tog

Round Robin

To make stockinette stitch when you knit in the round, you always knit on the right side, continuing around the circular or double-point needles without ever turning your work. (On straight needles, stockinette is created by knitting on one side, turning, and purling on the return.) For small projects like newborn hats and baby booties, use double-point needles to knit in the round; for larger tubes, use circular needles.

To knit with double-point needles, cast on the correct number of stitches for your project, and divide the stitches evenly among three of the needles (or as the pattern directs). Lay the work on a flat surface, forming the three needles into a triangle. Arrange the cast-on stitches so they are flat and all facing toward the center of the triangle. Look carefully along the needles and especially at

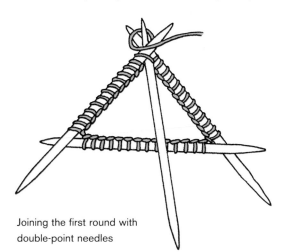

Joining the first round with double-point needles

- To avoid the common problem of loose stitches that develop where the needles change, make sure that each time you reach those corners you snug the yarn firmly after knitting the first stitch on the new needle. Another trick to keep the tension even is to move several stitches from one needle to the next after the first few rounds.
- To make it easier to handle your knitting, arrange your needles so the ends of the two you are working with lay on top of the third needle.
- After the first round is complete, check again to be sure no stitches have twisted around the needles. You want your finished project to be a nice tube, not a Mobius strip!
- Use a stitch marker, small safety pin, or piece of yarn in a different color to mark the first stitch of the round.
- Make sure that you never reverse direction when knitting in the round. Knitting clockwise will help you avoid this mistake.

the corners to make sure that the stitches don't take an extra twist around the needle.

The next step is the trickiest: Carefully lift the needles, keeping the stitches aligned, and use the working yarn that formed the last cast-on stitch to knit the first stitch on the left-hand needle. Snug the yarn firmly before knitting the second stitch. (Do not tie to join.) Knit across until the left-hand needle is empty. Use the empty needle to knit the stitches on the next needle. Continue knitting until the first round is complete. Place a marker or contrasting color yarn on the first stitch to indicate the beginning of each new round.

To knit with circular needles, cast on the correct number of stitches as usual, then lay the work on a flat surface. Arrange the stitches facing the center of the circle and carefully knit the first couple of stitches on the left-hand needle, taking care not to twist any stitches around the needles. Snug the yarn tightly between the last cast-on stitch and the first stitch in the first round. (Do not tie to join.) Place a marker between these two stitches to help you keep track of rounds.

Fun with Color

You can create an infinite number of fascinating designs by knitting with two or more colors in a single row or round. In this book, we illustrate color sequences in charts that are color-matched to the photos of the finished projects. Follow charts starting at the bottom line and read them from right to left on knit rows and from left to right on purl rows. We've placed a "start here" arrow on the charts as a reminder. If you use a different color scheme from ours, you may want to tape yarn swatches over the printed key to keep yourself on track.

When you knit with more than one color, carry the color or colors along on the wrong side, keeping the carried yarn loose so that it doesn't pucker the fabric. Don't carry the yarn for more than three stitches or you'll end up with long loops that can get snagged by baby's tiny and curious fingers. To avoid this, catch the carried yarn by wrapping the working yarn from beneath and around it every three or four stitches, as shown.

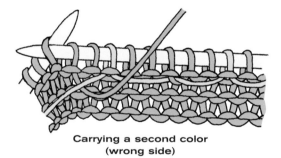

**Carrying a second color
(wrong side)**

When you change yarn colors, always take the color you want to emphasize from below the other (see facing page). On the front, the color handled this way will dominate the pattern and create a more uniform design. Be sure to take the same yarn, usually the darker one, consistently from below throughout the project.

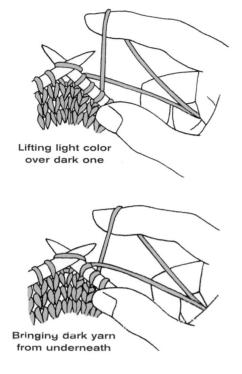

Lifting light color over dark one

Bringing dark yarn from underneath

If you are able to use one hand for one color and the other hand for a second color, you'll find that two-color knitting goes quickly and easily.

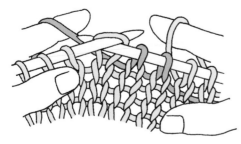

Two-handed color knitting

Joining New Yarn

When you run out of yarn and need to start a new end, it's best to do so toward the edge of the garment, where the join is less likely to be noticed. One way to join new yarn is to lay the new yarn over the old yarn so that you can knit the two together for three or four stitches, then drop the old yarn and continue with the new. When you come to those doubled stitches in the next row, be sure to knit the two yarns together as one. Be aware that if the yarn you're using is very smooth, plain, and/or inelastic, this kind of join may show.

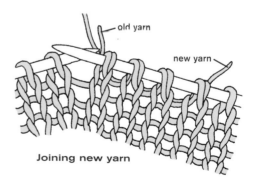

Joining new yarn

A less visible way to join new yarn is to catch a tail of the new yarn under the old yarn for six or seven stitches, then cut the old yarn and catch its tail for another six or seven stitches in much the same way you carry a second color in multi-color knitting.

Felting Instructions

Several projects in this book are felted after knitting. When wool fibers are subjected to hot water, soap, and agitation, a chemical and structural change occurs, which bonds the fibers. The result: a firm fabric that is durable, permanently shaped, and warm, even when wet. Bev Galeskas (Fiber Trends) shares advice on how to successfully felt hand-knit items:

1. Set washer on lowest water level, fill with hot water, and add a small amount of liquid dish detergent or rinse-free wool-wash, such as Wool Mix.

2. Place project in a zippered laundry bag or pillow cover. Including blue jeans helps increase agitation and speeds the process. Avoid towels or other items that may transfer lint to the knits.

3. Agitate. The amount of time needed for felting may vary. Monitor by checking every 5 minutes, then more frequently as items begin to felt. Set your washer back to continue the agitation until your project is felted to your liking. If you have a front-loading washer, you'll have less control, since you'll have to let it go through entire cycles.

4. When the knitting is felted as desired, remove it from the washer and rinse in cold water. Squeeze (don't twist) to remove the water. Using your washer's spin cycle is not recommended, as it may set a permanent crease in your felt. You can use a towel to take up excess. Firmly mold the item into shape. If possible, try the hat on the lucky owner. Poke your fingers inside booties to stretch them into shape.

5. Let the item dry for a couple of days. You should leave the hat over a bowl or other mold that maintains the desired size; you may wish to stuff the booties with paper toweling or plastic bags. The items may shrink a bit more as they dry, so keep checking and stretching, as needed.

6. To care for the finished item, hand wash it in lukewarm water, rinse, reshape it if necessary, and air-dry.

Baby Blocks

You may be anxious to see your beautiful new creation on baby's cute little head or feet, but do take the time to weave all loose ends in on the wrong side of the fabric, then block it properly. You'll be surprised at how any unevenness disappears when you block your knitting. Do not block chenille and ribbon yarns.

You can steam-block all-wool fabrics by holding a steam iron just above the surface so the steam penetrates the fabric, or cover the surface with a wet pressing cloth and lightly touch the iron to it. Either way, avoid pressing hard or moving the iron back and forth. Never iron or block a ribbed hem, as the process will cause it to lose its elasticity.

For wool blends, mohair, angora, alpaca, or cashmere, just dampen the knitted piece by spraying it lightly with water, then pin it to a flat surface where you can safely leave it to air-dry. Be sure to pin it so the dimensions are correct and the stitches are lined up straight.

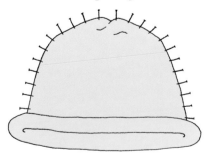

Blocking a finished hat

Seamly Seams

With a few exceptions, a simple running stitch is best for sewing together seams on hats, because it has the elasticity to match the hat's potential stretch.

1. Place the pieces to be seamed with the right sides together and pin them in place, with the edges neatly aligned.
2. Thread a blunt tapestry needle with the same yarn with which you knit the hat. Starting at the bottom edge, insert the needle from the top, leaving a 4-inch tail of yarn (you'll weave this in later).
3. Make small stitches just inside the edge stitches of the hat. Continue to the end. Weave the beginning and end tails of yarn through several knit stitches in the seam allowance. Cut the yarn.

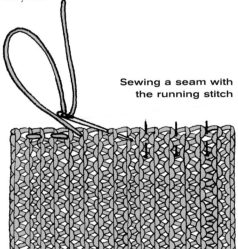

Sewing a seam with the running stitch

Finished Effects

You can always finish a hat with a plain crown, of course, but when you want to add a flourish to the top of a hat, here are several favorites: I-cords, pompoms, and tassels. Pompoms and tassels are sewn on after a project is complete. Make sure you attach these items extremely tightly! I-cords can be knitted as a continuous piece of the garment, so there is no risk of them coming off. Make sure you keep these short (4 inches maximum) so that they don't get caught around the baby's neck or end up in the baby's mouth.

Making a pompom or tassel: Steps 3 & 4

POMPOMS

These fuzzy balls can be as large or as small as you like. The following directions are for a standard size.

1. Cut a block of cardboard that is as wide as you want your pompom to be.
2. Wrap yarn around the cardboard 50–125 times, depending on the pompom's diameter

Making a pompom or tassel: Step 2

and the yarn's weight. Keep the strands evenly spaced and don't overlap them too much in the center.

3. Insert an 8-inch (20cm) length of yarn through one side of the wrapped yarn. Draw in the ends of the short yarn and knot them together.
4. Slide the tip of your scissors under the yarn at the opposite edge and cut through all the layers.
5. Remove the cardboard and trim the yarn edges to neaten.
6. Thread the ends of the knot through a needle and pull them to the inside of the hat. Tie them securely in a square knot and weave in the loose ends.

TASSELS

The method for making tassels is similar to that for pompoms. Tassels can be as short or as long as you like.

1. Cut a block of cardboard that is the length you want your tassel to be.
2. Wrap yarn around the cardboard 25 times for worsted weight or 15 times for bulky weight.
3. Insert an 8-inch (20cm) length of yarn under one side of the wrapped yarn. Draw in the ends of the short yarn and knot them together.
4. Slide the tip of your scissors under the yarn at the opposite edge and cut all the layers.
5. Wrap another 8-inch (20cm) length of yarn around the tassel 1 inch (2cm) below the previous knot, tie it tightly, and let the ends blend into the rest of the tassel.
6. Cut the loose ends to the same length.
7. Thread the yarn ends for the upper knot through a yarn needle and pull both into position on the hat. Tie them in a secure square knot inside the hat. Weave in the loose ends.

I-CORDS

I-cords are narrow tubes knitted on two double-point needles. The project directions will specify the number of stitches — usually 3 or 4.

1. Using double-point needles, cast on 3 (or 4) stitches; knit 3 (or 4).
2. Do not turn the needle. Instead, slide the stitches to the right hand end of the needle, so the first cast-on stitch is the first stitch at the tip of the left needle and the last stitch knitted is farthest away from tip. Insert the right needle, knitwise, into that stitch, bring the yarn from the left hand end across the back of the piece, wrap it around the right needle, and knit the stitch in the usual manner. Make sure you knit this stitch tightly.
3. Knit the 2 remaining stitches on the needle.
4. Repeat steps 2 and 3 until the I-cord is the desired length.

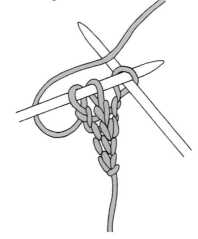

Knitting an I-cord

Bumblebee Socks

Designed by Barbara Telford, Woodsmoke Woolworks

Babies will be fascinated by these whimsical socks, which have bees knitted into the tops of the feet and still more bees dangling from the laces. Be sure to attach the dangles tightly enough that little fingers can't pry them loose. The wing and eye bobbles look complicated but they're actually simple to make — all you do is expand a stitch out to two or three stitches and then knit the stitches back together again.

Sizes and approximate finished lengths:

Infant small (0–3 months), 2¾" (7cm)

Infant medium (3–6 months), 3½" (9cm)

Yarn: Briggs & Little Regal, 100% wool, worsted weight

Small:

  20 yds (18m) mc (heathered purple)

  10 yds (9m) cc A (heathered lilac)

  10 yds (9m) cc B (yellow)

  10 yds (9m) cc C (brown)

Medium:

  30 yds (27m) mc (heathered purple)

  15 yds (14m) cc A (heathered lilac)

  15 yds (14m) cc B (yellow)

  15 yds (14m) cc C (brown)

Needles

One set #4 (3.5mm) dp needles

One set #6 (4.0mm) dp needles

One set #3 (3.0 or 3.25mm) straight needles

Gauge: 22 sts = 4" (10cm) on #6 (4.0mm) needles in St st

Other supplies: Yarn needle; crochet hook; small amount of stuffing, such as polyester fill

---

cc = contrasting color ◆ **dp** = double point ◆ **inc** = increase by knitting into the front and back of the next stitch ◆ **K** = knit ◆ **K2tog** = knit 2 stitches together ◆ **K3tog** = knit 3 stitches together **mc** = main color ◆ **P** = purl ◆ **P2tog** = purl 2 stitches together ◆ **ppso** = pass previous stitch over ◆ **rnd(s)** = round(s) ◆ **sl** = slip ◆ **ssk** = slip, slip, knit the 2 slipped stiches together **st(s)** = stitch(es) ◆ **St st** = stockinette stitch **W&T** = wrap and turn ◆ **yd(s)** = yard(s)

KNITTING THE CUFF	INFANT S	INFANT M
NOTE: The instructions given are for one sock. Left and right socks are identical. For advice about knitting with four dp needles, see Round Robin on pages 17–18.		
With #6 (4.0mm) dp needles and mc, cast on	26 sts	30 sts
Divide the sts among the 3 needles as follows:	8/10/10	10/10/10
*K1, P1; repeat from * until work measures	2" (5cm)	2.5" (6cm)
Change to #4 (3.5mm) needles and knit 1 rnd.		
MAKING EYELETS FOR LACING		
NOTE: Increases (inc) in this section are made by knitting into the front and back of the next stitch (see page 14).		
Round 1: K4, ppso, *K (see column at right), ppso; repeat from * 4 more times.	4 sts	5 sts
At the end of Round 1,	K2	K1
You will have	20 sts	24 sts
Round 2: K1, inc 1, *K (see column at right), inc 1; repeat from * 4 more times.	2 sts	3 sts
At the end of Round 2,	K3	K2
You will have	26 sts	30 sts
MAKING THE CHECKERBOARD RING AT THE ANKLE		
Round 1: *K1 in cc B, K1 in cc C; repeat from * to end of rnd.		
Round 2: *K1 in cc C, K1 in cc B; repeat from * to end of rnd.		

KNITTING THE HEEL FLAP	INFANT S	INFANT M
NOTE: The heel flap is knitted back and forth on two dp needles in stockinette st. Leave the remainder of the stitches on a spare needle until it is time to pick them up again. Continuing in the checkerboard pattern with cc B and cc C, knit	13 sts	15 sts
Turn and work in St st on these sts, beginning with a purl row, for	7 rows	9 rows
Next row: Change to cc A and knit 1 row.		
TURNING THE HEEL		
NOTE: See below, How to Wrap and Turn (W&T), for advice on turning the heel.		

How to Wrap and Turn (W&T)

The wrap and turn (W&T) method eliminates the small hole that appears when you turn in a middle of a row.

On Knit Rows:
1. Work up to the turning point; slip next stitch (purlwise) onto the right needle.
2. Move the yarn between the needles to the front of the work; return slipped stitch to the left needle.
3. Move the yarn between the needles to the back; turn to work in other direction. (W&T is complete.)

On Purl Rows:
1. Work up to the turning point; slip next stitch (purlwise) onto the right needle.
2. Move the yarn between the needles to the back of the work; return slipped stitch to the left needle.
3. Move the yarn between the needles to the front; turn to work in other direction. (W&T is complete.)

	INFANT S	INFANT M
Continuing to work back and forth on two needles with cc A, P (see column at right), P2tog, * W&T, sl 1, K4, ssk, W&T, sl 1, P4, P2tog; repeat from * until 6 sts remain on the needle.	8 sts	9 sts
Next row: Knit to end of row.		

KNITTING THE INSTEP

	INFANT S	INFANT M
NOTE: To work the bee on the instep, you will follow the Bee Band Chart for the appropriate size on page 30. See Making Bobbles on page 31 for instructions on making the bee's wings and eyes. Carry the cc yarn for the full round to avoid having loose ends to weave in. When the color changes from cc B to cc C or vice versa, simply drop the first color between Needles 1 and 2. See the illustration on page 31 for picking up sts along the heel flap.		
SET UP: Return to knitting in the round. The needle that has the 6 sts remaining from the heel turn is Needle 1. Use it to pick up from the side of the heel flap	8 sts	9 sts
Needle 2 has the stitches you held aside when you worked the heel.		
With Needle 3, pick up from the other side of the heel flap.	7 sts	8 sts
K3 from Needle 1 onto Needle 3.		
Needle 1 now has	11 sts	12 sts
Needle 2 now has	13 sts	15 sts
Needle 3 now has	10 sts	11 sts
Next Round Needle 1: With cc A, knit to last 3 sts, K2tog, K1. Needle 2: Work first row of Bee Band Chart for your size. Needle 3: With cc A, K1, ssk, knit to end.		

	INFANT S	INFANT M
Continue as above, decreasing 1 st at the end of the first and at the beginning of the third needles each rnd and following the bee pattern from the chart on Needle 2, until you have	26 sts	30 sts
Continue working even until the end of the pattern.		
Next Rounds: After finishing the Bee Band Chart, knit around the sock to the beginning of Needle 2 and begin a new round there. From this point on Needle 2 will be the first in the round and all needle names change accordingly.		
For medium size only: Knit 2 rnds in mc.		
Next Round: *K1 in cc B, K1 in cc C; repeat from * to end of rnd.		
Next Round: *K1 in cc C, K1 in cc B; repeat from * to end of rnd.		

SHAPING THE TOE

Round 1
Needle 1: Using mc, K1, ssk, knit to last 3 sts, K2tog, K1.

Needle 2: K1, ssk, knit to end.

Needle 3: Knit to last 3 sts, K2tog, K1.

Next rounds: Repeat Round 1 until you have 5 sts on Needle 1, 3 sts on Needle 2, and 2 sts on Needle 3.

Slip the sts from Needle 2 to Needle 3 and graft the toe with Kitchener Stitch (see page 89 for directions).

Cut the yarn and weave in loose ends.

MAKING THE BEE DANGLES

NOTE: Instructions are for one dangle. Make four dangles, two for each sock.

	INFANT S	INFANT M
With mc and #3 (3.25mm) needles, cast on 3 sts loosely.		
Row 1 (line 1, purl row): Inc 2 by knitting into the front, then the back, then the front of all 3 sts (see page 14). You will have 9 sts.		
Rows 2–5: Work in St st, following Bee Dangle Chart on page 31.		
Row 6 (line 6): K1, ssk, make wing bobble, K1, make wing bobble, K2tog, K1. You will have 7 sts.		
Row 7: K1, ssk, K1, K2tog, K1. You will have 5 sts.		
Row 8: K1, make eye bobble, K1, make eye bobble, K1.		
Row 9: K2tog, K1, K2tog. You will have 3 sts.		
Cut the yarn and pull it through the remaining sts. Sew the seams with the wrong sides together, leaving a hole for stuffing. Stuff the bee lightly and sew up the hole.		
MAKING THE LACES		
Insert the crochet hook into the nose of one bee dangle and, using mc, make 50 chains (see illustration and instructions on page 91). Cut the yarn, leaving a generous tail, and pull it through the last chain. Starting at the hole at the right side of the pattern, weave the chain through the eyelets. Attach the second bee dangle securely to the other end of the chain.		

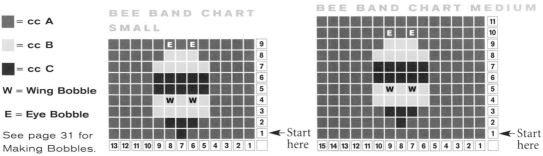

= cc A

= cc B

= cc C

W = Wing Bobble

E = Eye Bobble

See page 31 for
Making Bobbles.

BEE BAND CHART
SMALL

BEE BAND CHART MEDIUM

Picking Up Stitches

To pick up stitches, slide a crochet hook through the space just below the cast-off edge. Pull the yarn through and place a newly created stitch on the left-hand needle.

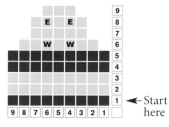

										9
	E		E							8
										7
	W		W							6
										5
										4
										3
										2
										1 ← Start here

| 9 | 8 | 7 | 6 | 5 | 4 | 3 | 2 | 1 | |

Making Bobbles

These socks feature bobbles knitted into the bee pattern and the dangles. Bobbles are made by knitting several stitches into a single stitch, working on these expanded stitches for one or more rows, and reducing them back into a single stitch.

To make the first wing bobble (W), with cc B knit 2 sts into the marked st. Work on these 2 sts in St st for 9 rows, starting and ending with purl rows, then K2tog through the back. Pick up and knit the st you originally knitted into, then pass the bobble st over it.

To make the second wing bobble (W), with cc B knit 2 sts into the marked st. Work on these 2 sts in St st for 10 rows, starting with a purl row, then P2tog through the back. Pick up and knit the st you originally knitted into, then pass the bobble st over it.

To make the eye bobble (E), with cc C knit 3 sts into the marked st (knit into the front, back, and front again). Turn and P3, then turn again and K3tog through the back. Pick up and knit the st you originally knitted into, then pass the bobble st over it.

Baby Beret

Designed by Nancy Lindberg, Circle Pines, MN

You don't have to live on the banks of the Seine to love this classic beret. From its elegant picot edge to the crocheted flower on the brim, the beret has flair — yet it's fast and easy to knit, since it's all in stockinette stitch. The hats pictured here are knit in cotton yarns similar in weight to worsted wool, but directions are also given for lightweight fingering yarn. You'll find that this hat looks great in almost any yarn.

cc = contrasting color ◆ **dp** = double point
K = knit ◆ **K2tog** = knit 2 stitches together
inc = increase ◆ **mc** = main color
M1 = make one ◆ **rnd(s)** = round(s)
st(s) = stitch(es) ◆ **ssk** = slip, slip, knit the 2 slipped stitches together ◆ **St st** = stockinette stitch ◆ **YO** = yarn over

Sizes: Small (3–6 months), 14" (35cm)
Medium (9–12 months), 16" (40cm)

Worsted Weight Version (shown at right)
Top
Yarn: Brown Sheep Cotton Fleece, 80% pima cotton/20% merino wool
  80 yds (72m) mc (Banana)
  10 yds (9m) cc A (Nymph)
  25 yds (23m) cc B (Banana)
Needles
One set #5 (3.75mm) dp needles
One set #6 (4mm) dp needles
Bottom
Yarn: Classic Elite Spotlight, 100% cotton
  80 yds (72m) mc (blue/#5708)
  10 yds (9m) cc A (white/#5701)
  25 yds (23m) cc B (lilac/#5756)
Needles
One set #3 (3.25mm) dp needles
One set #4 (3.5mm) dp needles
Gauge for worsted weight version
20 sts = 4" on larger needles in St st

Fingering Weight Version
140 yds (126m) mc; 10 yds (9m) cc A; 25 yds (23m) ccB
Needles for fingering weight version
One set #2 (2.75mm) dp needles
One set #3 (3.25mm) dp needles
Gauge for fingering weight version: 28 sts = 4" (10cm) on #3 (3.25mm) needles in St st
Supplies: Yarn needle, 4E or 6G crochet hook

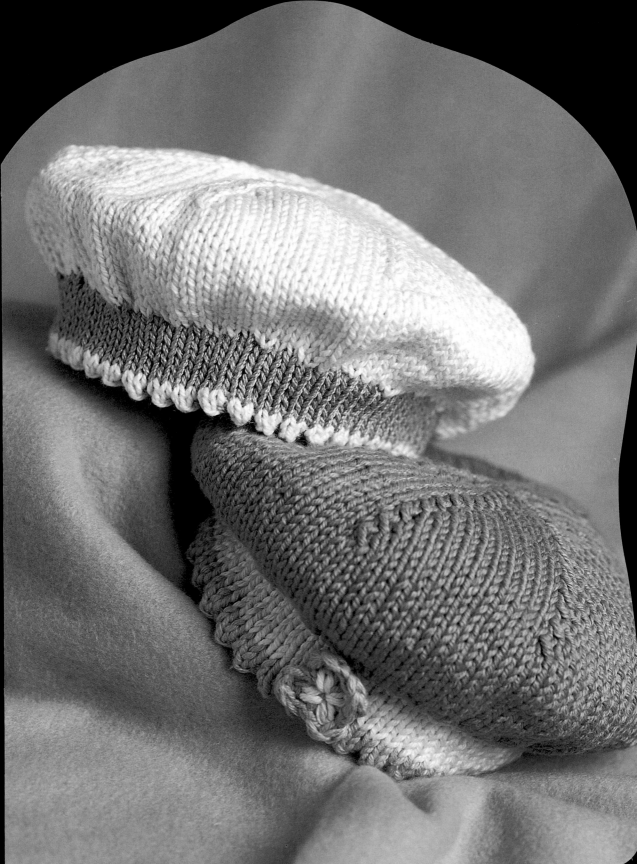

KNITTING THE HEM	SMALL (FINGERING)	MEDIUM (FINGERING)	SMALL (WORSTED WT)	MEDIUM (WORSTED WT)
NOTE: For advice about knitting with four dp needles, see Round Robin on pages 17–18.				
With smaller dp needles and cc B, cast on	102 sts	108 sts	72 sts	78 sts
Distribute the sts evenly among the needles.				
Work in St st (knit every round) until measurement from cast-on edge is	1" (2.5cm)	1¼" (5cm)	1" (2.5cm)	1¼" (5cm)
KNITTING THE CUFF				
Round 1: *K2tog, YO; repeat from * to end of rnd to make a picot edge. You will still have the same number of sts on the needles as you cast on.				
Next Rounds: Knit 3 more rounds with cc B.				
Change to cc A, and continue to knit in rounds until measurement from picot edge is	1" (2.5cm)	1¼" (3cm)	1" (2.5cm)	1¼" (3cm)
KNITTING THE TOP OF THE HAT				
Round 1: Change to mc. *K3, M1; repeat from * to end of rnd. You will have	136 sts	144 sts	96 sts	104 sts
Change to dp needles (see column at right)	#3	#3	#5	#5
Knit even in St st for	2¼" (5.5cm)	2½" (6.5cm)	2¼" (5.5cm)	2½" (6.5cm)
DECREASING FOR THE TOP				
Round 1: *K (see column at right), ssk; repeat from * 7 more times.	15 sts	16 sts	10 sts	11 sts
You will have	128 sts	136 sts	88 sts	96 sts

	SMALL (FINGERING)	MEDIUM (FINGERING)	SMALL (WORSTED WT)	MEDIUM (WORSTED WT)
Round 2 and all other even-numbered rnds: Knit to end of rnd.				
Round 3: K (see column at right), ssk; repeat from * 7 more times.	14 sts	15 sts	9 sts	10 sts
Continue in St st, decreasing 8 sts in each odd rnd, with one fewer st between decreases each time, until you have 16 sts remaining.				
FINISHING				
Cut the yarn, leaving a 12" tail to draw through the remaining sts and fasten off.				
Fold the beret on the picot edge, and tack the cast-on edge to the inside.				
If desired, crochet a flower (see instructions below), or make a pompom (see page 22 for instructions) and sew it to the top of the hat.				

The Crocheted Flower for the Band

Round 1: Using cc B, work 4 chain stitches, and join with a slip stitch to the first chain to form a ring. Leave a 3-inch tail.

Round 2: Chain 3, * 1 chain in ring, 2 double chains in ring, 1 chain in ring; repeat from * 3 times. Chain 2, slip stitch at the bottom of the chain 3 to join and fasten off, leaving a 3-inch tail. With cc A, work a lazy daisy stitch at the center of the flower. Position the flower in the center of the band, and fasten it to the hat. Weave any ends inside the band.

Simply Chenille

Designed by Lynda Gemmell, Cabin Fever

Chenille is made from layers of woven fabric cut into very narrow strips. It's beautifully soft and richly colored, but it isn't as stretchy as yarns made from spun fiber, so the hat should be sized generously. If you want to substitute a spun yarn, you'll probably need a #8 (5.0mm) needle to achieve the same gauge. The acryllic chenille shown here should be hand-washed and then laid flat to dry. Manufacturers of most cotton chenille yarns also recommend handwashing with warm water and laying item flat to dry. Check yarn label for specific instructions.

Sizes and circumferences

Infant (0–6 months), 17" (43cm)

1 year, 18" (45cm)

Yarn: Velvet Chenille by Sweaterkits. com, 100% acrylic, worsted weight, emerald green (#3198) or navy (#3180)

Infant: 80 yds (72m)

1 year: 90 yds (81m)

Needles

One set #6 (4.0mm) dp needles

One #6 (4.0mm) circular needle, 16" (40cm) long

One #10 (6.0mm) straight needle

Gauge: 16 sts = 4" (10cm) on #6 (4.0mm) needles in St st

Other supplies: Yarn needle, safety pin

---

dp = double point ◆ **K** = knit
mc = main color ◆ **M1** = make 1 stitch
rnd(s) = round(s) ◆ **st(s)** = stitch(es)
St st = stockinette stitch ◆ **yd(s)** = yard(s)

MAKING THE I-CORD	INFANT	1 YEAR
With dp needles and mc, cast on 4 sts. Using two needles, make a 1" (2.5cm) I-cord. (See I-cord instructions on page 23.)		
After the last round, redistribute the sts onto two dp needles so you can knit with the third needle. Mark the beginning of the round by putting a safety pin through the first st in the round. **NOTE:** For more advice about knitting with four dp needles, see Round Robin on pages 17–18.		
INCREASING FOR THE TOP OF THE HAT		
Round 1: *K1, M1; repeat from * to end of rnd. You will have	8 sts	8 sts
Redistribute your stitches onto three needles so you can knit with the fourth needle. Change to the circular needle when you can.		
Rounds 2–5: Knit even in St st.		
Round 6: *K1, M1; repeat from * to end of rnd. You will have	16 sts	16 sts
Rounds 7–10: Knit even in St st.		
Round 11: *K1, M1; repeat from * to end of rnd. You will have	32 sts	32 sts
Rounds 12–15: Knit even in St st.		
Round 16: *K2, M1; repeat from * to end of rnd. You will have	48 sts	48 sts
Rounds 17–20: Knit even in St st.		
Round 21: *K3, M1; repeat from * to end of rnd. You will have	64 sts	64 sts
Rounds 22–25: Knit even in St st.		
Round 26: *K (see column at right), M1; repeat from * to end of rnd.	16 sts	8 sts
You will have	68 sts	72 sts

KNITTING THE BRIM AND FINISHING UP	INFANT	1 YEAR
Knit even in St st for	5" (12.5cm)	5¾" (14.5cm)
Use the #10 (6.0mm) straight needle to cast off, then sew in the ends. Sew in the end of the cast-off round on the right side so it won't show when the brim is rolled up.		

Felted Flapped Derby

Designed by Cindy Walker, Stony Hill Fiberarts

Felting helps this derby keep its shape and makes it warm and weatherproof. The earflaps make it even warmer. You can use a contrasting color or a different yarn for the flaps, or even make the derby without them. The hat pictured here is knitted in a mohair/wool blend, giving it a fuzzy texture, but any untreated animal fiber would work as well. Double-knit or sport yarn can be used for a smaller, lighter-weight hat.

Sizes and finished circumferences:

Small (3–12 months), 16"–18" (40.5cm– 45.5cm)

Medium (1–2 years), 18"–19" (45.5cm–48cm)

Large (2–3+ years), 19"–20" (48cm–51cm)

Yarn: Henry's Attic, 55% mohair/45% wool, hand-dyed by the designer, or other natural fiber in worsted or double-knit weight that provides the correct gauge

NOTE: For information on other yarns suitable for felting, see Felting Tips on page 45.

Small: 110 yds (99m) mc plus 22 yds (20m) mc or cc for earflaps

Medium: 150 yds (135m) mc plus 22 yds (20m) mc or cc for earflaps

Large: 200 yds (180m) mc plus 22 yds (20m) mc or cc for earflaps

Needles

One set #10½ (6.5mm) dp needles

One #10½ (6.5mm) circular needle, 16" (40.5cm) long

Gauge: 14 sts = 4" (10cm) on #10½ (6.5mm) needles in St st

Other supplies: Yarn needle, cc thread for marking

---

cc = contrasting color ◆ **dp** = double point ◆ **K** = knit ◆ **K2tog** = knit 2 stitches together **inc** = increase ◆ **mc** = main color ◆ **rnd(s)** = round(s) **st(s)** = stitch(es) ◆ **St st** = stockinette stitch ◆ **yd(s)** = yard(s)

From: _____

BUSINESS REPLY MAIL

FIRST-CLASS MAIL   PERMIT NO. 10   N. ADAMS MA

POSTAGE WILL BE PAID BY ADDRESSEE

STOREY BOOKS

PO Box 206
North Adams MA 01247-9919

We'd love your thoughts . . .

Your reactions, criticisms, things you did or didn't like about this Storey Book. Please use space below (or write a letter if you'd prefer
— even send photos!) telling how you've made use of the information . . . how you've put it to work . . . the more details the better!
Thanks in advance for your help in building our library of good Storey Books.

Book Title: _____

Purchased From: _____

Comments: _____

_____

_____

_____

_____

Pamela B. Art

President, Storey Books

Your Name: _____
(Please Print)

Mailing Address: _____

E-mail Address: _____

☐ You have my permission to quote from my comments and use these quotations in ads, brochures, mail, and other promotions used
to market Storey Books.

To order this book or any Storey title CALL 800-441-5700 or visit our web site at www.storey.com

Signed _____ Date _____

e-mail: feedback@storey.com   website: www.storey.com

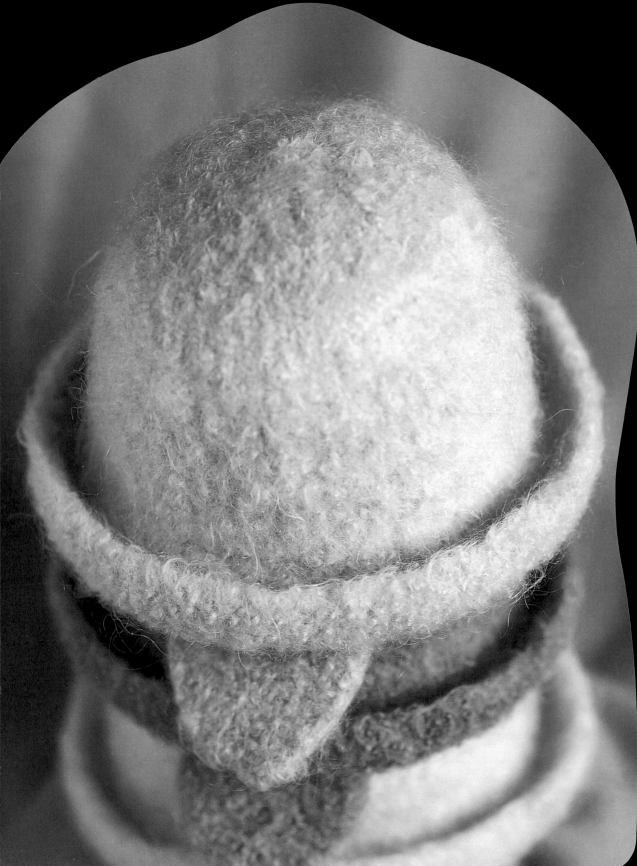

KNITTING THE HAT BRIM	SMALL	MEDIUM	LARGE
NOTE: For advice about knitting in the round, see Round Robin on pages 17–18.			
With the #10½ (6.5mm) circular needle, cast on	80 sts	100 sts	110 sts
Round 1: Join (do not twist stitches). Knit to end of rnd.			
Round 2: *K9, inc 1 in next st; repeat from * to end of rnd. You will have	88 sts	110 sts	121 sts
Rounds 3–6: Knit to end of each rnd.			
Round 7: *K9, K2tog; repeat from * to end of rnd. You will have	80 sts	100 sts	110 sts
Rounds 8 and 9: Knit to end of each rnd.			
Round 10: *K8, K2tog; repeat from * to end of rnd. You will have	72 sts	90 sts	99 sts
Rounds 11–13: Knit to end of each rnd. (You can knit a few additional rounds if you want a brim that is larger than the one shown in the picture.)			
MAKING THE SIDES			
Round 14: *K2tog, K1; repeat from * to end of rnd. You will have	48 sts	60 sts	66 sts
Round 15: *K (see column at right), inc 1 in next st; repeat from * to end of rnd.	3 sts	9 sts	5 sts
You will have	60 sts	66 sts	77 sts
For large size only, extra round: K76, inc 1 in next st. You will have			78 sts
Next round: Knit to end of rnd.			

	SMALL	MEDIUM	LARGE
Next round: You will be knitting a short length of a contrasting color yarn into the work as a marker thread in two places to indicate the starting points for the earflaps (see page 45):			
Knit	13 sts	15 sts	21 sts
Knit a length of marker thread along with the working yarn for	21 sts	21 sts	21 sts
Knit	5 sts	9 sts	15 sts
Knit a length of marker thread as before for	21 sts	21 sts	21 sts
Continue knitting in St st until the distance from the marker threads is	7" (18cm)	8" (20.5cm)	8" (20.5cm)
DECREASING FOR THE TOP			
NOTE: Change to dp needles when necessary.			
Round 1: *K4, K2tog; repeat from * to end of rnd. You will have	50 sts	55 sts	65 sts
Rounds 2, 4, 6, and 8: Knit to end of each rnd.			
Round 3: *K3, K2tog; repeat from * to end of rnd. You will have	40 sts	44 sts	52 sts
Round 5: *K2, K2tog; repeat from * to end of rnd. You will have	30 sts	33 sts	39 sts
Round 7: *K1, K2tog; repeat from * to end of rnd. You will have	20 sts	22 sts	26 sts
Round 9: *K2tog; repeat from * to end of rnd. You will have	10 sts	11 sts	13 sts
Round 10: *K2tog; repeat from * to end of rnd (K1 at ends of rnds for larger two sizes). You will have	5 sts	6 sts	7 sts

	SMALL	MEDIUM	LARGE
Draw the yarn end through the remaining sts and fasten off on the inside. Weave in all the loose ends. Work the loose end at the beginning into the right side, so it will be hidden behind the brim.			
KNITTING THE EARFLAPS			
Working on the underside of the hat, pick up 21 sts below one of the marker threads, inserting the needle into the lower loop of each st (see illustration on page 45). These are the sts for the earflap. Work back and forth, turning at the end of each row. The earflap will look like the illustration on page 45.			
Rows 1, 3, and 5: Knit to end of each row.			
Row 2: K1, K2tog, K15, K2tog, K1. You will have	19 sts	19 sts	19 sts
Row 4: K1, K2tog twice, K9, K2tog twice, K1. You will have	15 sts	15 sts	15 sts
Row 6: K1, K2tog, K9, K2tog, K1. You will have	13 sts (7 ridges)	13 sts (7 ridges)	13 sts (7 ridges)
Rows 7–15: Knit to end of each row.			
Row 16: K1, K2tog, K7, K2tog, K1. You will have	11 sts	11 sts	11 sts
Rows 17, 19, 21, and 23: Knit to end of each row.			
Row 18: K1, K2tog, K5, K2tog, K1. You will have	9 sts	9 sts	9 sts
Row 20: K1, K2tog, K3, K2tog, K1. You will have	7 sts	7 sts	7 sts
Row 22: K1, K2tog, K1, K2tog, K1. You will have	5 sts	5 sts	5 sts
At the end of Row 23, you will have 11 ridges. Cast off all sts, cut the yarn, and weave in the loose ends. Remove the marker thread.			

	SMALL	MEDIUM	LARGE
Work the second earflap in the same way.			
FELTING			
Felt the hat, following the Felting Instructions on page 20.			

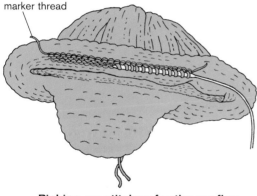

marker thread

Picking up stitches for the earflap

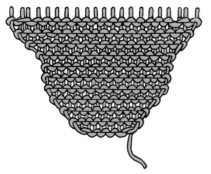

Knitting the earflap

Felting Tips

Any animal fiber, such as wool, alpaca, and mohair, will felt, as long as it hasn't been treated. Washable (superwash) wool, bleached white wool, cotton, rayon, silk, and synthetic fibers don't felt. Many off-white and light colors do not felt well, if at all. Before jumping into your project, be sure to knit a swatch with the yarns you've chosen, and then felt the swatch following the directions on page 20. Measure before and after felting, so that you can estimate the finished size of your project more accurately. It's not unusual to find that different colors of the same yarn felt differently. Some take longer than others, or they may not even achieve the degree of felting desired. Always test knit!

FELTED FLAPPED DERBY

Make Way for Ducklings

Designed by Barbara Telford, Woodsmoke Woolworks

Celebrate spring with a hat that has it all: a row of ducklings parading around the edge, two rows of duck eggs, and still more ducklings dangling from the crown. Be sure to attach the ducklings tightly enough so that little fingers can't pry them off. Working in five colors and three dimensions in a small space is a challenge, but the results are well worth it.

Sizes and finished circumferences:

Small (3 months), 15½" (39cm)

Medium (6 months), 17½" (44cm)

Yarn: Brown Sheep Lamb's Pride Superwash, 100% wool, worsted weight

Small:

   130 yds (117m) mc (Misty Blue)

   30 yds (27m) cc A (Alabaster)

   7 yds (6m) cc B (Saffron)

   1 yd (1m) cc C (Onyx)

Medium:

   160 yds (144m) mc (Misty Blue)

   40 yds (36m) cc A (Alabaster)

   10 yds (9m) cc B (Saffron)

   1 yd (1m) cc C (Onyx)

Needles

One set #4 (3.5mm) dp needles

One set #6 (4.0mm) dp needles

Gauge: 22 sts = 4" (10cm) on #6 (4.0mm) needles in St st

Other supplies: Yarn needle; crochet hook; small amount of stuffing, such as polyester fill

---

cc = contrasting color ◆ **dp** = double point ◆ **inc** = increase ◆ **K** = knit ◆ **K2tog** = knit 2 stitches together ◆ **K3tog** = knit 3 stitches together ◆ **K4tog** = knit 4 stitches together ◆ **mc** = main color ◆ **P** = purl ◆ **P2tog** = purl 2 stitches together ◆ **psso** = pass slip stitch over **rnd(s)** = round(s) ◆ **sl** = slip ◆ **ssk** = slip, slip, knit the 2 slipped stitches together ◆ **st(s)** = stitch(es) ◆ **St st** = stockinette stitch ◆ **yd(s)** = yard(s)

KNITTING THE HEM	SMALL	MEDIUM
NOTE: For advice about knitting with four dp needles, see Round Robin on pages 17–18.		
With #4 (3.5mm) needles and mc, cast on	72 sts	80 sts
Work in K1, P1 ribbing for	3" (7.5cm)	3.5" (9cm)
KNITTING THE SIDES		
Change to #6 (4.0mm) needles and knit even for 2 rnds with mc.		
Change to cc B and work the pattern in St st by following Duck Band Chart for your size on page 50. Start with line 1 at the bottom of the chart, and work from right to left. See Making Bobbles on page 51 for instructions for the egg bobbles. Going around the hat, you will have	9 ducks	10 ducks
Change yarn to mc.		
For medium size: Knit even for 2 rnds.		
DECREASING FOR THE TOP		
Round 1: *K (see column at right), ssk; repeat from * to end of rnd.	7 sts	8 sts
You will have	64 sts	72 sts
Round 2: *K (see column at right), ssk; repeat from * to end of rnd.	6 sts	7 sts
You will have	56 sts	64 sts
Continue in the same way, decreasing 8 sts in every rnd until you have	16 sts	16 sts
Next rnd: *Ssk; repeat from * to end of rnd. You will have	8 sts	8 sts
Next rnd: *Ssk; repeat from * to end of rnd. You will have	4 sts	4 sts
Cut the yarn and pull it through the remaining sts. Close the hole and weave in any loose ends. Fold ribbed hem to inside and sew into place.		

KNITTING THE DUCKLING DANGLES	SMALL	MEDIUM
The dangles are knitted separately and attached to the hat. You can make as many as you like. Follow the Duckling Dangle Chart on page 50. See Making Bobbles on page 51 for instructions for making their beaks, wings, and tail feathers. For instructions on how to increase (inc), see page 14. We are calling the cast-on row "Row 1" so that rows and lines on chart correspond.		
Row 1: With cc A and #4 (3.5mm) needles, cast on	3 sts	3 sts
Row 2 (knit row): Inc 1, inc 2, inc 1. You will have	7 sts	7 sts
Row 3 (purl row): P2, P1 with cc C, P1, P1 with cc C, P2.		
Row 4: K3, with cc B, make beak bobble, K3.		
Rows 5, 7, and 9: Purl to end of each row.		
Row 6: Inc 1 in each of the first 3 stitches, K1, inc 1 in each of the next 3 stitches. You will have	13 sts	13 sts
Row 8: K3, make wing bobble, K5, make wing bobble, K3.		
Row 10: Knit to end of row.		
Row 11: P4, P2tog, P1, P2tog, P4. You will have	11 sts	11 sts
Row 12: Make two tail feathers, K2tog, sl 1, K2tog, psso, K2tog, make two tail feathers. You will have	7 sts	7 sts
Row 13: P2tog, sl 1, P2tog, psso, P2tog. You will have	3 sts	3 sts
Cut the yarn and pull it through the remaining sts, leaving a 6" tail.		
FINISHING THE DUCKLING DANGLES		
Weave in the loose ends from the eyes and bobbles. Fold in half with the right sides together and sew the seam, leaving a hole at the bottom for stuffing. Stuff lightly and sew the hole closed.		

MAKING THE TASSEL	SMALL	MEDIUM
Put the crochet hook through the st at the top of the head. Fold in half a 3' (1m) piece of mc yarn, and catch it in the middle with the crochet hook. Using both sides of the yarn as one piece, crochet 12 chains (see page 91 for illustration and instructions on making chain sts). Pull one end of the yarn through the last chain to fasten off. Pull both ends of the yarn through the hole in the top of the hat, and with a yarn needle, use the ends to sew the dangle to the top of the hat.		

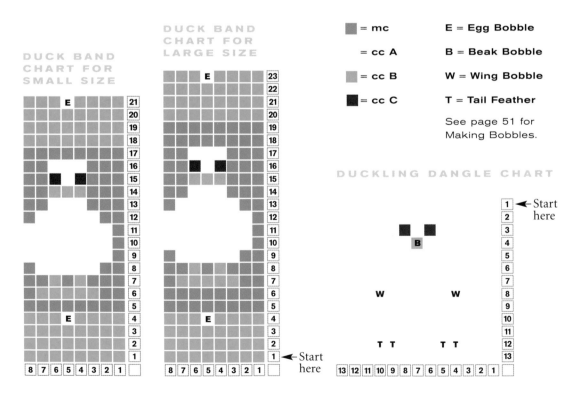

DUCK BAND CHART FOR SMALL SIZE

DUCK BAND CHART FOR LARGE SIZE

= mc
= cc A
= cc B
= cc C

E = Egg Bobble
B = Beak Bobble
W = Wing Bobble
T = Tail Feather

See page 51 for Making Bobbles.

DUCKLING DANGLE CHART

Making Bobbles

This hat features bobbles knitted into the pattern band and into the duckling dangles. Bobbles are made by knitting several stitches into a single stitch, working on these expanded stitches for one or more rows, and reducing them back into a single stitch.

To make the egg bobbles (E) in the pattern band, change to cc A and knit 4 sts into the marked st (knit into the front, back, and front and back again). Turn the work and P4, then turn it again and K4tog through the back. With cc B, pick up and knit the st you originally knitted into, then pass the bobble st over it.

For the beak bobble (B), change to cc B and knit 2 sts into the marked st. Work on these 2 sts in St st for 3 rows, ending with a purl row, then K2tog through the back. With cc A, pick up and knit the st you originally knitted into, then pass the bobble st over it.

For the wing bobbles (W), continue in cc A and knit 3 sts into the marked st. Turn and work on these 3 sts in St st for 3 rows, ending with a purl row, then K3tog through the back. Pick up and knit the st you originally knitted into, then pass the bobble st over it.

The tail feathers (T) look like loops rather than bobbles, but they are worked in essentially the same way. Continuing in cc A, knit the tail st, then sl it knitwise to the left needle and knit it again 12 more times. Pick up and knit the st you originally knitted into, then pass the tail st over it.

Felted Fooshies

Designed by Cindy Walker, Stony Hill Fiberarts

You may not find "fooshies" in the dictionary, but you'll find them on the feet of the best-dressed babies. What else would you call these soft, warm slippers with stretchy cuffs? The straps are optional, and so are the suede soles. Felting helps them keep their shape — you knit them oversize, then wash them in hot water until they reach the size you want.

Sizes and approximate finished lengths:

Small (3–12 months), 4" (10cm)

Medium (12–18 months), 5" (12.5cm)

Large (18–30 months), 6" (15cm)

NOTE: Exact finished lengths depend on yarn and point at which you stop felting.

Yarn: Henry's Attic, 55% mohair/45% wool, hand-dyed by the designer, or other natural animal fiber in worsted or double-knit weight that can be felted and that will provide the correct gauge (see Felting Tips, page 45)

Small: 70 yds (63m) mc (pink), 16 yds (14m) cc A (blue); Medium: 85 yds (77m) mc (pink), 18 yds (16m) cc A (blue); Large: 122 yds (110m) mc (pink), 22 yds (20m) cc A (blue)

Elasticized cotton: Cascade Fixation

Small: 26 yds (23m) cc B (white); Medium: 31 yds (28m) cc B (white); Large: 36 yds (32m) cc B (white)

NOTE: For cuff, use any yarn that will not felt.

Needles

One set #3 (3.25mm) dp needles

One #10½ (6.5mm) circular needle, 16" (40.5cm) long

Gauge

Wool: 13 sts = 4" (10cm) on #10½ (6.5mm) needles in St st, before felting

Cotton: 28 sts = 4" (2.5cm) on #3 (3.25mm) needles in St st

Other supplies: Yarn needle, stitch holder, marker thread in contrasting color, button, suede or leather for sole, nylon thread for attaching sole

---

cc = contrasting color ◆ **dp** = double point ◆ **inc** = increase ◆ **K** = knit **K2tog** = knit 2 stitches together ◆ **mc** = main color ◆ **P** = purl ◆ **P2tog** = purl 2 stitches together ◆ **psso** = pass slip stitch over ◆ **rnd(s)** = round(s) ◆ **sl** = slip **st(s)** = stitch(es) ◆ **St st** = stockinette stitch ◆ **yd(s)** = yard(s)

KNITTING THE SOLES	SMALL	MEDIUM	LARGE
NOTE: The instructions given are for one sole. Left and right soles are identical. See the illustration on page 55. Increases are made by knitting two stitches into one stitch.			
With the #10½ (6.5mm) circular needle and mc, cast on	3 sts	6 sts	7 sts
Row 1 and all odd-numbered rows: Knit to end of each row.			
Row 2 (right side): K1, inc 1, then	inc 1	K4	K3, inc 1, K1
You will have	5 sts	7 sts	9 sts
Row 4: K1, inc 1, knit to last 2 sts, inc 1, K1. You will have	7 sts	9 sts	11 sts
Row 6: K1, inc 1, knit to last 2 sts, inc 1, K1. You will have	9 sts	11 sts	13 sts
Row 8: K1, inc 1, knit to last 2 sts, inc 1, K1. You will have	11 sts	13 sts	15 sts
Row 10: K1, inc 1, knit to last 2 sts, inc 1, K1. You will have	13 sts	15 sts	17 sts
For medium and large sizes only, Row 12: K1, inc 1, knit to last 2 sts, inc 1, K1. You will have	(13 sts)	17 sts	19 sts
For all sizes: Continue knitting in garter st to the end of	Row 29	Row 35	Row 41
On the right side of the work, you will have	15 ridges	18 ridges	21 ridges
First decrease row: K1, K2tog, knit to last 3 sts, K2tog, K1. You will have	11 sts	15 sts	17 sts
Continue knitting in garter st to the end of	Row 35	Row 41	Row 53
On the right side of the work, you will have	18 ridges	21 ridges	27 ridges
Second decrease row: K1, K2tog, knit to last 3 sts, K2tog, K1. You will have	9 sts	13 sts	15 sts

	SMALL	MEDIUM	LARGE
Continue knitting in garter st, decreasing 2 sts every other row until 3 sts remain. On the right side of work, you will have	22 ridges	27 ridges	33 ridges
Last row: Sl 1 knitwise, K2tog, psso. Leave the final st loose.			
KNITTING THE SIDES			
Keeping the final st on the needle, go around the outer edge of the sole, picking up additional sts by slipping the outermost loop of each ridge onto the needle. Make sure sts are evenly spaced so the fooshie will not be lopsided. You will have	45 sts	57 sts	69 sts

At-a-Glance Construction

These drawings will help you visualize some of the trickier construction techniques.

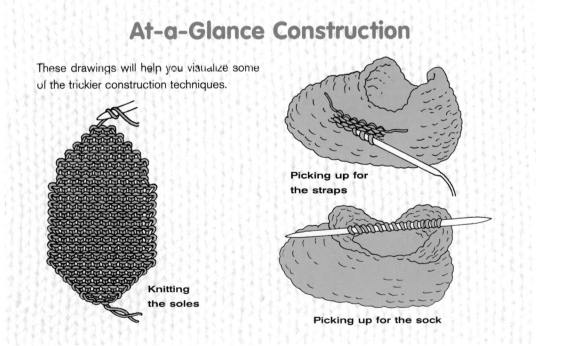

Knitting the soles

Picking up for the straps

Picking up for the sock

	SMALL	MEDIUM	LARGE
Mark the first st (back of heel) and the center st (front of toe).			
NOTE: For advice about knitting with four dp needles, see Round Robin on pages 17–18.			
Continue knitting in the round in garter st, by purling one round, knitting one round, purling one round, and so on, beginning with a purl round, for	3 rnds	3 rnds	3 rnds
Round 4 *For small size:* K17, *K2tog, K1; repeat from * 2 more times. K2tog, K17. You will have *For medium size:* K21, *K2tog, K1, K2tog; repeat from * 2 more times. K21. You will have *For large size:* K26, *K2tog, K1; repeat from * 4 more times. K2tog, K26. You will have	41 sts	51 sts	63 sts
Round 5: Purl to end of rnd.			
Round 6 *For small size:* K17, K2tog, K3, K2tog, K17. You will have *For medium size:* K21, K2tog twice, K1, K2tog twice, K21. You will have *For large size:* K26, *K2tog, K1; repeat from * 2 more times. K2tog, K26. You will have	39 sts	47 sts	59 sts
Round 7: Purl to end of rnd.			
NOTE: In this round you will work a length of contrasting color yarn along with your working yarn. The contrasting yarn is a marker yarn that establishes the starting level for the strap.			
For the right fooshie, carry marker yarn from	st 11 to st 18	st 13 to st 21	st 16 to st 25

	SMALL	MEDIUM	LARGE
For the left fooshie, carry marker yarn from	st 22 to st 29	st 27 to st 35	st 35 to st 44

Round 8

For small size: *K3, K2tog; repeat from * 2 more times. K2, K2tog, K1, K2tog, K2, *K2tog, K3; repeat from * 2 more times. You will have

For medium size: *K3, K2tog; repeat from * 3 more times. *K1, K2tog; repeat from * 2 more times. *K3, K2tog; repeat from * 2 more times, K3. You will have

For large size: K4, K2tog, *K3, K2tog; repeat from * 3 more times. *K1, K2tog; repeat from * 2 more times. *K3, K2tog; repeat from * 3 more times, K4. You will have

	SMALL	MEDIUM	LARGE
Round 8	31 sts	37 sts	47 sts

Round 9

For small size: P10, P2tog, *P1, P2tog; repeat from * 2 more times, P10. You will have

For medium size: P12, P2tog, P1, P2tog, P3, P2tog, P1, P2tog, P12. You will have

For large size: P16, P2tog, P3, P2tog, P1, P2tog, P3, P2tog, P16. You will have

	SMALL	MEDIUM	LARGE
Round 9	27 sts	33 sts	43 sts

Round 10: Knit to end of rnd.

Round 11

For small size: P2, P2tog, P4, P2tog, *P1, P2tog; repeat from * 2 more times. P4, P2tog, P2. You will have

For medium size: P2, P2tog, P6, P2tog, P2, P2tog, P1, P2tog, P2, P2tog, P6, P2tog, P2. You will have

For large size: P5, P2tog, P8, P2tog, P2, P2tog, P1, P2tog, P2, P2tog, P8, P2tog, P5. You will have

	SMALL	MEDIUM	LARGE
Round 11	21 sts	27 sts	37 sts

KNITTING THE HEELS	SMALL	MEDIUM	LARGE
Row 1: Continuing with the stitches on the needle in Round 11, knit	7 sts	9 sts	13 sts
Row 2: Turn and knit	14 sts	18 sts	24 sts
Slide the unused sts onto a stitch holder. You will now be knitting in rows, turning the work after each row.			
Row 3: Changing to cc, knit to end of row.			
Row 4: Cast off 1 st and knit to end of row. You will have	13 sts	17 sts	23 sts
Row 5: Cast off 1 st and knit to end of row. You will have	12 sts	16 sts	22 sts
Row 6: Cast off 1 st, then *For small size:* K3, K2tog, K5. You will have *For medium size:* K2, *K2tog, K4; repeat from * 1 more time. You will have *For large size:* *K3, K2tog; repeat from * 2 more times, K5. You will have	10 sts	13 sts	18 sts
Row 7: Cast off 1 st, knit to end of row. You will have	9 sts	12 sts	17 sts
Cast off remaining sts.			
KNITTING THE TONGUES			
TIP: You can start from either side of the work. Move from the stitch holder back to the needle	7 sts	9 sts	13 sts
Row 1: With mc, K1, inc 1, knit to last 2 sts, inc 1, K1. You will have	9 sts	11 sts	15 sts
Row 2: Knit to end of row.			

	SMALL	MEDIUM	LARGE
Row 3 *For small size:* K1, K2tog, K3, K2tog, K1. You will have	7 sts		
For medium size: K1, K2tog, K5, K2tog, K1. You will have		9 sts	
For large size: K1, inc 1, K2, K2tog, K3, K2tog, K2, inc 1, K1. You will have			15 sts
Row 4 *For small and medium sizes:* Knit to end of row. *For large size:* K2tog, K11, K2tog. You will have			13 sts

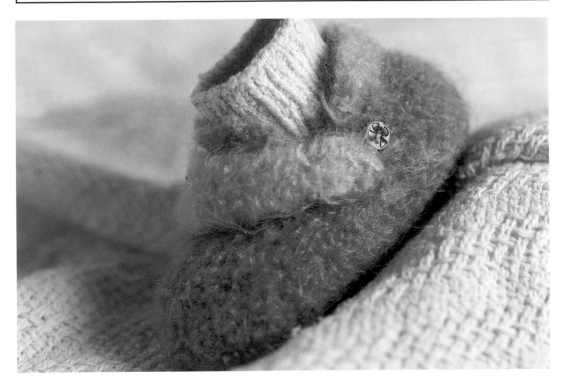

	SMALL	MEDIUM	LARGE
Row 5 *For small size:* K2tog, K3, K2tog. Cast off remaining 5 sts. *For medium size:* K1, inc 1, K5, inc 1, K1. You will have *For large size:* Knit to end of row.		11 sts	
Row 6 *For medium size:* Knit to end of row. *For large size:* K2tog, K1, K2tog, K3, K2tog, K1, K2tog. You will have			9 sts
Row 7 *For medium size:* *K2tog, K1; repeat from * 2 more times, K2tog. Cast off remaining 7 sts. *For large size:* Knit to end of row.			
For large size only, Row 8: K2tog, K5, K2tog. Cast off remaining 7 sts.			
MAKING THE STRAP FOR THE RIGHT FOOSHIE			
NOTE: The strap is joined on the left for the right fooshie, and on the right for the left fooshie.			
Working from heel to toe with cc A, pick up (see column at right) from the lower loops of the ridge below the marker row. Pick up an additional 2 sts from the lower loop of the ridge below that one. See the illustration on page 55.)	4 sts	5 sts	5 sts
You will have	6 sts	7 sts	7 sts
Starting at the toe end with a purl row, work in St st for	8 rows	10 rows	10 rows
Next row: P1, P2tog, purl to end of row. You will have	5 sts	6 sts	6 sts

	SMALL	MEDIUM	LARGE
Continue working in St st for	5 rows	5 rows	7 rows
Next row: P1, P2tog, purl to end of row. You will have	4 sts	5 sts	5 sts
Continue working in St st for	5 rows	5 rows	5 rows
Next row: P1, P2tog,	P1	P2	P2
For medium and large sizes only: Continue working in St st for		5 rows	5 rows
Next row: P1, P2tog, P1. You will have		3 sts	3 sts
For large size only: Continue working in St st for			4 rows
For all sizes: Sl 1 st knitwise, K2tog, psso. Tie off, sew in loose ends, and remove the marker thread.			
MAKING THE STRAP FOR THE LEFT FOOSHIE			
Working from heel to toe with cc A, pick up (see column at right) from the lower loop of the ridge below the marker row. Pick up an additional 2 sts from the lower loop of the ridge below that one. (See illustration on page 55.)	4 sts	5 sts	5 sts
You will have	6 sts	7 sts	7 sts
Starting at the toe end with a knit row, work in St st for	8 rows	10 rows	10 rows
Next row: K1, K2tog, knit to end of row. You will have	5 sts	6 sts	6 sts
Continue working in St st for	5 rows	5 rows	7 rows
Next row: K1, K2tog, knit to end of row. You will have	4 sts	5 sts	5 sts
Continue working in St st for	5 rows	5 rows	5 rows

	SMALL	MEDIUM	LARGE
Next row: K1, K2tog,	K1	K2	K2
For medium and large sizes only: Continue working in St st for		5 rows	5 rows
Next row: K1, K2tog, K1. You will have		3 sts	3 sts
For large size only: Continue working in St st for			4 rows
For all sizes: Sl 1 st purlwise, P2tog, psso. Tie off, sew in loose ends, and remove the marker thread.			

MAKING THE SOCKS

	SMALL	MEDIUM	LARGE
With dp needles, pick up sts along the top of the fooshie, on the inside, starting at the center of the heel (see illustration page 55) as follows:			
Needle 1 Starting at center back, along the top of the heel, pick up	5 sts	9 sts	11 sts
Between the heel and tongue, pick up	4 sts	4 sts	4 sts
Inside the tongue, (below the top), pick up	3 sts (2 ridges)	3 sts (3 ridges)	3 sts (5 ridges)
You will have	12 sts	16 sts	18 sts
Needle 2 From the tongue, pick up	4 sts	5 sts	11 sts
Between tongue and heel, pick up	4 sts	4 sts	4 sts
Needle 3 Along the top of the heel to the center back where you began, pick up	8 sts	9 sts	11 sts
Needle 1 has Needle 2 has Needle 3 has	12 sts 8 sts 8 sts	16 sts 9 sts 9 sts	18 sts 15 sts 11 sts

	SMALL	MEDIUM	LARGE
Using cc B, knit clockwise in St st for 4 rnds, adjusting the number of sts on each needle to spread them more evenly, if desired.			
Change to K1, P1 ribbing for 1.5" (4cm) or more, if desired.			
Bind off loosely and sew in all loose ends. Pull out all marker threads still remaining.			
FELTING			
Felt the fooshies, following the Felting Instructions on page 20. While they are drying, tug gently on the straps to get them to the right length.			
FINISHING			
Sew on a button to hold down the strap loop.			

Safe, No-Slip Soles

To keep toddlers from slipping, you may want to sew on a suede or leather sole. Place the dried and shaped fooshie on a scrap of suede and draw around the edge (or make a paper pattern first, if you wish). Cut out the suede sole and sew it to the fooshie with nylon thread using an overcast stitch. Or, do it the easy way: Use two-sided fusible webbing, and simply iron the layers together, following the webbing label instructions.

Felted High-Tops

Designed by Cindy Walker, Stony Hill Fiberarts

These high-top booties are made from one multicolor skein of yarn, which the designer dyes in the specific lengths needed, but you could create the same effect using several different yarn colors. The booties are built from the sole up, then you add the sides, the heel, and finally the tongue. Felting helps the booties keep their shape, so they're snug and warm without being tight. The finished high-top looks like something a pixie might wear.

Sizes and approximate lengths:

Small (3–8 months), 4.5" (11.5cm)

Medium (8–18 months), 5" (12.5cm)

NOTE: Exact finished length will be determined by the yarn and the point at which you stop felting.

Yarn: Henry's Attic, 55% mohair/45% wool, hand-dyed by the designer, or other natural animal fiber in worsted or double-knit weight, or any yarn that can be felted and that will provide the correct gauge

NOTE: For information on other yarns suitable for felting, see Felting Tips on page 45.

Small: 40 yds (36m) mc (turquoise), 20 yds (18m) cc A (seafoam), 40 yds (36m) cc B (lilac)

Medium: 50 yds (45m) mc (turquoise), 30 yds (27m) cc A (seafoam), 50 yds (45m) cc B (lilac)

Needles: One #10½ (6.5mm) circular needle, 16" (40.5cm) long

Gauge: 13 sts = 4" (10cm) on #10½ (6.5mm) needles in St st, before felting

Other supplies: Yarn needle, 2 stitch markers, stitch holder, suede or leather for sole, nylon thread for attaching sole

---

cc = contrasting color ◆ **dp** = double point ◆ **inc** = increase ◆ **K** = knit ◆ **K2tog** = knit 2 stitches together ◆ **M1** = make 1 ◆ **mc** = main color ◆ **P** = purl ◆ **P2tog** = purl 2 stitches together ◆ **psso** = pass slip stitch over ◆ **rnd(s)** = round(s) ◆ **sl** = slip ◆ **st(s)** = stitch(es) ◆ **St st** = stockinette stitch ◆ **yd(s)** = yard(s)

KNITTING THE SOLES	SMALL	MEDIUM
NOTE: The instructions given are for one sole. Left and right soles are identical. See the illustration on page 54. For how to increase (inc), see page 14.		
With the #10½ (6.5mm) circular needle and cc A, cast on	3 sts	6 sts
Row 1 and all odd-numbered rows: Knit to end of each row.		
Row 2 (right side): K1, inc 1, then	inc 1	K4
You will have	5 sts	7 sts
Row 4: K1, inc 1, knit to last 2 sts, inc 1, K1. You will have	7 sts	9 sts
Row 6: K1, inc 1, knit to last 2 sts, inc 1, K1. You will have	9 sts	11 sts
Row 8: K1, inc 1, knit to last 2 sts, inc 1, K1. You will have	11 sts	13 sts
Row 10: K1, inc 1, knit to last 2 sts, inc 1, K1. You will have	13 sts	15 sts
For medium size only, Row 12: K1, inc 1, knit to last 2 sts, inc 1, K1. You will have		17 sts
For both sizes: Continue knitting in garter st to the end of	Row 29	Row 35
On the right side of the work, you will have	15 ridges	18 ridges
First decrease row: K1, K2tog, knit to last 3 sts, K2tog, K1. You will have	11 sts	15 sts
Continue knitting in garter st to the end of	Row 35	Row 41
On the right side of the work, you will have	18 ridges	21 ridges
Second decrease row: K1, K2tog, knit to last 3 sts, K2tog, K1. You will have	9 sts	13 sts
Continue knitting in garter st, decreasing 2 sts every other row as before until 3 sts remain. On the right side of the work, you will have	22 ridges	27 ridges
Last row: Sl 1 st knitwise, K2tog, psso. Leave the final st loose.		

KNITTING THE SIDES	SMALL	MEDIUM
Keeping the final st from the sole on the needle, go around the outer edge, picking up additional sts by slipping the outermost loop of each ridge onto the needle. Make sure sts are evenly spaced so the bootie will not be lopsided. You will have	45 sts	57 sts
Mark the first st (back of heel) and the center st (front of toe).		
NOTE: For advice about knitting with four dp needles, see Round Robin on pages 17–18.		
Rounds 1–3: With cc A, knit in the round in garter st (purl 1 round, knit 1 round, purl 1 round, and so on), beginning with a purl rnd.		
Round 4 *For small size:* K17, * K2tog, K1; repeat from * 2 more times, K2tog, K17. You will have *For medium size:* K21, * K2tog, K1, K2tog; repeat from * 2 more times, K21. You will have	41 sts	51 sts
Round 5: Purl to end of rnd.		
Round 6 *For small size:* K17, K2tog, K3, K2tog, K17. You will have *For medium size:* K21, K2tog twice, K1, K2tog twice, K21. You will have	39 sts	47 sts
Round 7: Purl to end of rnd.		
Round 8 *For small size:* K2, K2tog, * K3, K2tog; repeat from * 2 more times. K1, K2tog, * K3, K2tog; repeat from * 2 more times, K2. You will have *For medium size:* * K3, K2tog; repeat from * 3 more times. *K1, K2tog; repeat from * 2 more times. *K3, K2tog; repeat from * 2 more times, K3. You will have	31 sts	37 sts

SHAPING THE TONGUES	SMALL	MEDIUM
Slide onto the left needle the last	8 sts	9 sts
Cut the yarn from the sole and join cc B, leaving a 4" (10cm) tail. To make the tongue, you will be turning after each row instead of knitting in the round. Turn bootie over and knit toward the toe.		
Row 1: Knit	15 sts	19 sts
Slide onto a stitch holder the remaining	16 sts	18 sts
Rows 2 and 4: K1, M1, K (see column at right), * K2tog, K1; repeat from * 2 more times. K2tog, K (see column at right), M1, K1.	1 st	3 sts
You will have	13 sts	17 sts
Rows 3 and 5: K1, M1, knit to last st, M1, K1. You will have	15 sts	19 sts
Row 6: K1, M1, (see column at right), M1, K1.	* K3, K2tog; repeat from * one more time, K3	K4, K2tog, K5, K2tog, K4
You will have	15 sts	19 sts
Row 7: K1, M1, knit to last st, M1, K1. You will have	17 sts	21 sts
Row 8: K1, M1, (see column at right), M1, K1.	K5, K2tog, K1, K2tog, K5	K6, K2tog, K3, K2tog, K6
You will have	17 sts	21 sts
Row 9: K1, M1, knit to last st, M1, K1. You will have	19 sts	23 sts
Row 10: K1, M1, knit to last st, M1, K1. You will have	21 sts	25 sts
Rows 11 and 13: Knit to end of each row.		

	SMALL	MEDIUM
Rows 12 and 14: K1, M1, (see column at right), M1, K1.	K7, K2tog, K1, K2tog, K7	K9, K2tog, K1, K2tog, K9
For medium size only, Row 15: Knit to end of row.		
Cast off all sts.		
SHAPING THE HEELS		
Pick up the sts from the stitch holder. Join cc B on the right back of the bootie, leaving a 4" (10cm) tail. You are still turning after each row.		
Row 1: Knit.		
For medium size only, extra row: K1, M1, K16, M1, K1. You will have		20 sts
Row 2: K1, M1, (see column at right), M1, K1.	K5, (K2tog) twice, K5	K6, K2tog, K2, K2tog, K6
You will have	16 sts	20 sts
Row 3: K1, M1, knit to last st, M1, K1. You will have	18 sts	22 sts
Row 4: K1, M1, K1, M1, (see column at right), M1, K1, M1, K1.	K3, K2tog, (K1, K2tog) twice, K3	K4, K2tog, (K2, K2tog) twice, K4
You will have	19 sts	23 sts
Row 5: K1, M1, knit to last st, M1, K1. You will have	21 sts	25 sts
Row 6: K1, M1, (see column at right), M1, K1.	K6, K2tog, K3, K2tog, K6	K8, K2tog, K3, K2tog, K8
You will have	21 sts	25 sts

	SMALL	MEDIUM
Row 7: K (see column at right), * M1, K3; repeat from * 2 more times. M1, K (see column at right).	6 sts	8 sts
You will have	25 sts	29 sts
Rows 8 and 9: Knit to end of each row.		
Row 10: K1, M1, (see column at right), M1, K1.	K9, K2tog, K1, K2tog, K9	K10, K2tog, K3, K2tog, K10
You will have	25 sts	29 sts
Row 11: Knit to end of row.		
Row 12: K1, M1, (see column at right), M1, K1.	K5, K2tog, K2, K2tog, K1, K2tog, K2, K2tog, K5	K7, K2tog, K2, K2tog, K1, K2tog, K2, K2tog, K7
You will have	23 sts	27 sts
Row 13: Knit to end of row.		
Row 14: With mc, K1, M1, knit to last st, M1, K1. You will have	25 sts	29 sts
Row 15: Knit to end of row and cast off all sts.		
Using the tails that you left when you joined the yarn, sew up each side between the tongue and heel back to within 1" (2.5cm) of the top (or approximately 4 ridges from the top). Sew in all the loose ends.		
FELTING AND FINISHING		
Felt the booties, following the Felting Instructions on page 20.		
To keep toddlers from slipping, you may want to sew on a suede or leather sole (see instructions on page 63).		

Jester Hat

Designed by Deb Gemmell, Cabin Fever

Who could keep from smiling at this whimsical jester's hat? The jester points, with their stripes and bells, were traditional wear for the "motley fool" in centuries past and still have the power to charm us today. In this hat, the brim is knitted first, then all three jester points are knitted at the same time. The points are then cast off separately, and bells are attached to the ends. The garter stitch cuff provides the stockinette body with a nice contrasting texture.

Sizes and circumferences:

Small (0–6 months), 16½" (41.5cm)

Medium (12–18 months), 18½" (47cm)

Yarn: Tahki Cotton Classic, 100% cotton, double-knit weight (picture at right)

> **NOTE:** The hat on page 77 was knit with Patons Country Garden, 100% machine-washable merino wool, in Red Pennant, Deep Navy, and Snowdrop.

Small: 45 yds (40m) mc (#3936), 50 yds (45m) cc A (#3351), 50 yds (45m) cc B (#3463)

Medium: 50 yds (45m) mc (#3936), 70 yds (63m) cc A (#3351), 70 yds (63m) cc B (#3463)

Needles

One set #6 (4.0mm) dp needles

One #6 (4.0mm) circular needle, 16" (40cm) long

Gauge: 22 sts = 4" (10cm) on #6 (4.0mm) needles in St st

Other supplies: Yarn needle, 3 jingle bells, 6 stitch markers

---

cc = contrasting color ◆ **dp** = double point ◆ **K** = knit ◆ **inc** = increase ◆ **mc** = main color
P = purl ◆ **rnd(s)** = round(s) ◆ **p2sso** = pass 2 slip stitches over ◆ **sl** = slip ◆ **st(s)** = stitch(es) ◆ **St st** = stockinette stitch ◆ **W&T** = wrap and turn ◆ **yd(s)** = yard(s)

KNITTING THE HAT BRIM	SMALL	MEDIUM
NOTE: For advice about using circular needles, see Round Robin on pages 17–18.		
With the #6 (4.0mm) circular needle and mc, cast on	144 sts	160 sts
Round 1 (right side): Purl to end of rnd.		
Rounds 2, 4, 6, 8, 10, and 12: Knit to end of each rnd.		
Round 3: P6, *sl2 knitwise, with yarn at back of work, K1, p2sso, P13; repeat from *, ending the round with P7 instead of P13. You will have	126 sts	140 sts
Round 5: P5, *sl2 knitwise, with yarn at back of work, K1, p2sso, P11; repeat from *, ending with P6 instead of P11. You will have	108 sts	120 sts
Round 7: P4, *sl2 knitwise, with yarn at back of work, K1, p2sso, P9; repeat from *, ending with P5 instead of P9. You will have	90 sts	100 sts
Round 9: P4, *K1, P9; repeat from *, ending with P5 instead of P9.		
Rounds 11 and 13: Purl to end of rnd.		
Round 14: Purl to end of rnd, W&T. (See page 27 for instructions.)		
Rounds 15–19: Knit to end of each rnd.		
Round 20: Knit to end of rnd. *For medium size only:* Inc 2 sts evenly spaced. You will have	90 sts	102 sts
MAKING THE STRIPE PATTERN		

The remainder of the hat is knit in stripes of:
   3 rnds cc A
   3 rnds cc B		

	SMALL	MEDIUM
NOTE: To make a smooth transition from one color to the next, sew in the loose ends on the diagonal, as shown on page 121. The tails from the beginnings of the stripes are sewn up and to the left, while the tails from the ends of the stripes are sewn down and to the right. This trick gets rid of the "jog" where a new color starts.		
MAKING THE JESTER POINTS		
Work even in St st stripe pattern for	2" (5cm)	2" (5cm)
Marker Round: Continuing with the stripe pattern, place markers as follows: *For small only:* K11, *place marker, K8, place marker, K22; repeat from * once; place marker, K8, place marker, K11. *For large only:* K13, *place marker, K8 place marker, K26; repeat from * once; place marker, K8, place marker K13.		
Next round: K to marker, * M1, sl marker, K8, sl marker, M1, K to next marker; repeat from * 2 more times, the last time knitting to the end of the rnd.		
You will have	96 sts	108 sts
Continue in the same way, increasing 6 sts in each rnd, until a stripe is completed and the measurement from the beginning of the stripe pattern (measuring between the jester points) is	3" (7.5cm)	3½" (9cm)
For the next stripe only (garter stitch band): Round 1: K to marker, * M1, sl marker, K8, sl marker, M1, K to next marker; repeat from * 2 more times, the last time knitting to the end of the rnd.		

	SMALL	MEDIUM
Rounds 2 and 3: P to marker, * M1, sl marker, K8, sl marker, M1, P to next marker); repeat from * 2 more times, the last time purling to the end of the rnd.		
Continue as before, knitting all rnds and increasing 6 sts in each rnd until a stripe is completed and measurement from the beginning of the stripe pattern is	4½" (11.5cm)	5½" (14cm)
SHAPING THE TOP OF THE HAT		
Next round: With mc, knit to end of rnd.		
Turn the hat inside out and sl all the sts that are on the left needle from where the round began to the first marker, plus 4 sts past the marker, onto a dp needle. (Retain the markers.)		
Sl the same number of sts (the next group in the first jester point) onto a second dp needle.		
Using the three-needle cast-off technique described on page 13, cast off until only the markers and the 8 sts between them remain on the needles. Cut the yarn, leaving a tail of 8" (20cm). Remove the markers, thread the tail through the last 8 sts, and secure the end. Leave the remainder of tail loose and use it later to attach the bell.		
Cast off the other two jester points in the same way, working from the center out.		
At each jester point, attach a bell very securely to the right side with the remaining yarn tail. Be sure to test the security of the bells often, especially after washing, and re-attach them if they seem at all loose. Sew in the ends and close up the hole at the center top of the hat. Turn up the brim and sew in the cast-on end so it doesn't show. Tack hem in place.		

Kyle's Kap

Designed by Beverly Galeskas, Fiber Trends

To give them a bit more body, the visor and band for this cap are knitted with a double strand of yarn, while the rest of the hat is knitted with a single strand. The visor must be knitted tightly to keep it from flopping. Make sure the cast-on edge of the band can stretch enough to fit the child's head; if it doesn't, try using a larger needle for the cast-on. The topknot is simply a coiled I-cord knit in the same color as the visor and band.

Sizes and circumferences:
Small (3–6 months), 17" (43cm)
Medium (6–18 months), 19" (48cm)
Large (18–48 months), 21" (53cm)
Yarn: Crystal Palace Cotton Chenille, 100% cotton, worsted weight
Small: 110 yds (99m) mc (red)
Medium: 130 yds (117m) mc (red)
Large: 155 yds (140m) mc (red)
NOTE: If you want to knit the cap in one color and the brim in a contrasting color, as in the hat on page 83, use three-fifths of the yardage for mc and two-fifths for cc.

Needles
One set #7 (4.5mm) dp needles
One #7 (4.5mm) circular needle, 16" (40.5cm) long

Gauge
18 sts = 4" (10cm) on #7 (4.5mm) needles in St st
13 sts = 3½" (9cm) on #7 (4.5mm) needles in garter st with double yarn, stretching to between 4½" and 5" (11.5 to 12.5mm)
Other supplies: Yarn needle, stitch holder

---

cc = contrasting color ◆ **dp** = double point ◆ **K** = knit ◆ **K2tog** = knit 2 stitches together
inc = increase ◆ **mc** = main color ◆ **rnd(s)** = round(s) ◆ **ssk** = slip, slip, knit 2 together
st(s) = stitch(es) ◆ **St st** = stockinette stitch ◆ **yd(s)** = yard(s)

KNITTING THE VISOR	SMALL	MEDIUM	LARGE
NOTE: Leave about 3 yds of yarn as a "tail" when casting on.			
With the #7 (4.5mm) circular needle and two strands of mc or cc, cast on	30 sts	34 sts	38 sts
Row 1: Ssk, K (see column at right), K2tog, turn.	26 sts	30 sts	34 sts
You will have	28 sts	32 sts	36 sts
Row 2: K2tog, K (see column at right), ssk, turn.	24 sts	28 sts	32 sts
You will have	26 sts	30 sts	34 sts
Continue in garter st, decreasing 2 sts each row as in Rows 1 and 2, until you have	8 sts	8 sts	8 sts
Next row: K2tog, K2tog, ssk, ssk. You will have	4 sts	4 sts	4 sts
Slide the remaining 4 sts onto a holder and cut yarn.			
KNITTING THE VISOR EDGE			
Using the double-stranded "tail" left from the cast on, pick up sts along the side of the visor — 1 st per garter ridge, including the cast-on edge, for a total of	7 sts	8 sts	9 sts
Work across the 4 sts on the holder as follows: K1, K2tog, K1.			
Along the other side of the visor, pick up	7 sts	8 sts	9 sts
You will have	17 sts	19 sts	21 sts
NOTE: Because the knitting is tight, you may find a crochet hook useful for picking up stitches (see illustration on page 31).			
Slide all the visor sts back onto the stitch holder.			

KNITTING THE BAND	SMALL	MEDIUM	LARGE
With the #7 (4.5mm) circular needle and two strands of mc or cc, cast on	17 sts	18 sts	19 sts
With the right side facing you, knit across all the visor sts from the stitch holder.			
Cast on an additional (see column at right) and turn.	17 sts	18 sts	19 sts
You will have	51 sts	55 sts	59 sts
Next 5 rows: Knit to end of each row and turn. At the end of the last row, cut one of the strands of yarn. If making a two-color hat, cut the contrast yarn and join a single strand of mc.			
NOTE: From this point on, you will be knitting in the round with a single strand of mc.			
KNITTING THE SIDES OF THE HAT			
Increase row: Since the last row is worked with a double strand of yarn, an easy way to increase in a stitch is to knit each strand of yarn separately. *Small size:* *K1, inc in each of next 2 sts; repeat from * to last 3 sts, end K1, inc in next st, K1. You will have	84 sts		
Medium size: *K1, inc in each of next 2 sts; repeat from *, ending with K1. You will have		91 sts	
Large size: Inc in first st, *K1, inc in each of next 2 sts; repeat from *, ending with K1. You will have			98 sts
Do not turn. Join into round, making sure band is straight on needle. (For advice on knitting in the round, see Round Robin on pages 17–18.)			
Knit even in rounds of St st until work measures (see column at right) from top of band.	1½" (4cm)	1¾" (4.5cm)	2" (5cm)

DECREASING FOR THE CROWN	SMALL	MEDIUM	LARGE
NOTE: When the rounds become too small for the circular needle, switch to dp needles.			
Round 1: *K (see column at right), ssk; repeat from * to end.	10 sts	11 sts	12 sts
You will have	77 sts	84 sts	91 sts
Round 2 and all even rounds: Knit to end of each rnd.			
Round 3: *K (see column at right), ssk; repeat from * to end.	9 sts	10 sts	11 sts
You will have	70 sts	77 sts	84 sts
Continue decreasing on the odd-numbered rnds, with one fewer st between decreases each time, until 7 sts remain.			
Cut yarn and, with a yarn needle, thread it through the 7 sts; pull tight and fasten off.			
MAKING THE TOPKNOT			
NOTE: If you prefer, you can make the topknot with cc yarn (see photo on page 83).			
With #7 (4.5mm) dp needles and mc or cc, cast on	3 sts	3 sts	3 sts
Make a 2" I-cord, then cut the yarn, leaving at least 8", and thread the yarn through the cord with a yarn needle. (For instructions on how to make I-cords, see page 23.)			
Coil the cord tightly and fasten it securely to the top of the cap with the end of the yarn and a yarn needle.			
NOTE: Sew around the edge of the coiled cord and sew it securely through the center so the baby cannot chew or pull off the knot.			

FINISHING THE HAT	SMALL	MEDIUM	LARGE
Using a yarn needle, sew the short seam in the back of the band. Work in all the ends of the yarn.			
Block the cap by rinsing it in warm water and rolling it in a towel to remove excess water. Shape it over a small bowl or ball and smooth the visor flat on a tabletop. Allow it to air-dry.			

Ladybug Socks

Designed by Barbara Telford, Woodsmoke Woolworks

Legend has it that ladybugs are a sign of good luck, and any baby with a pair of these socks is lucky indeed! Red-and-black ladybugs crawl across the feet and dangle from the laces, and their color scheme is echoed in a checkerboard pattern around the ankles, heels, and toes. Making such complex patterns on a small item isn't easy, but it's worth going to the trouble for such beautiful results.

Sizes and finished lengths:
Infant small (0–3 months), 2¾" (7cm)
Infant medium (3–6 months), 3½" (9cm)
Yarn: Briggs & Little Regal, 100% wool, worsted weight
Small:
 20 yds (18m) mc (heathered pink)
 10 yds (9m) cc A (pink)
 10 yds (9m) cc B (red)
 10 yds (9m) cc C (black)
Medium:
 30 yds (27m) mc (heathered pink)
 15 yds (14m) cc A (pink)
 15 yds (14m) cc B (red)
 15 yds (14m) cc C (black)

Needles
One set #4 (3.5mm) dp needles
One set #6 (4.0mm) dp needles
One set #3 (3.0 or 3.25mm) straight needles
Gauge: 22 sts = 4" on #6 (4.0mm) needles in St st
Other supplies: Yarn needle; crochet hook; small amount of stuffing, such as polyester fill

---

cc = contrasting color ◆ **dp** = double point ◆ **inc** = increase ◆ **K** = knit ◆ **K2tog** = knit 2 stitches together ◆ **mc** = main color ◆ **P** = purl ◆ **P2tog** = purl 2 stitches together **ppso** = pass previous stitch over ◆ **rnd(s)** = round(s) ◆ **sl** = slip ◆ **ssk** = slip, slip, knit 2 together ◆ **st(s)** = stitch(es) ◆ **St st** = stockinette stitch ◆ **W&T** = wrap and turn **yd(s)** = yard(s)

KNITTING THE CUFF	INFANT S	INFANT M
NOTE: The instructions given are for one sock. Left and right socks are identical. All increases are made by knitting 2 stitches into 1 stitch.		
For advice about knitting with dp needles, see Round Robin, on pages 17–18.		
With #6 (4.0mm) needles and mc, cast on	26 sts	30 sts
Divide the sts evenly among three needles.		
*K1, P1; repeat from * until work measures	2" (5cm)	2.5" (6cm)
Change to #4 (3.5mm) needles and knit 1 rnd.		
MAKING EYELETS AND CHECKERBOARD		
Round 1: K4, ppso, *K (see column at right), ppso; repeat from * to end of rnd, ending with K (see column at right).	4 sts 2 sts	5 sts 1 st
You will have	20 sts	24 sts
Round 2: K1, inc 1, *K (see column at right), inc 1; repeat from * to end of rnd, ending with K (see column at right)	2 sts 3 sts	3 sts 2 sts
Break off mc yarn. You will have	26 sts	30 sts
Round 3: *K1 with cc B, K1 with cc C; repeat from * to end of rnd.		
Round 4: *K1 with cc C, K1 with cc B; repeat from * to end of rnd. These two rounds establish a checkerboard pattern that is continued in the heel.		
KNITTING THE HEEL FLAP		
Continuing in the checkerboard pattern with cc B and cc C, knit the heel stitches:	13 sts	15 sts

	INFANT S	INFANT M
Turn and continue to work the checkerboard pattern in St st on these sts, beginning with a purl row, for	7 rows	9 rows
Next row: Change to cc A and knit 1 row. Break cc B and cc C.		
TURNING THE HEEL		
NOTE: See page 27, How to Wrap and Turn (W&T), for instructions.		
Continuing to work on two needles with cc A, P (see column at right), P2tog, * W&T, sl 1, K4, ssk, W&T, sl 1, P4, P2tog; repeat from * until 6 sts remain on the needle.	8 sts	9 sts
Next row: Knit to end of row.		
KNITTING THE INSTEP		
NOTE: When you work on the Ladybug Band Chart on page 90, start with Line 1 at the bottom of the chart, and work from right to left. Carry the cc yarns for the full round to avoid having a large number of loose ends to weave in. When the color changes from cc B to cc C or vice versa, simply drop the first color between Needles 1 and 2.		
You will now return to knitting in the round. Pick up and distribute stitches as follows: With the needle that has the 6 sts remaining from the heel (Needle 1), pick up (see column at right) from the side of the heel flap. Knit the stitches you haven't been working on onto Needle 2. With Needle 3, from the other side of the heel flap, pick up	8 sts / 7 sts	9 sts / 8 sts
K3 from Needle 1 onto Needle 3.		
You will have Needle 1: Needle 2: Needle 3:	11 sts / 13 sts / 10 sts	12 sts / 15 sts / 11 sts

	INFANT S	INFANT M

Next Round
   Needle 1: With cc A, knit to last 3 sts, K2tog, K1.
 	
   Needle 2: Work first row of Ladybug Band Chart.
 	
   Needle 3: With cc A, K1, ssk, knit to end.		

Continue as above, decreasing 1 st on Needles 1 and 2 each rnd and following the Ladybug Band Chart on Needle 2, until you have	26 sts	30 sts
Continue working even until the end of the pattern.		
Next Rounds: After finishing the Ladybug Band Chart, knit around the sock to the beginning of Needle 2 and begin a new round there. **NOTE:** From this point on, all needles are renamed, starting here as Needle 1.		
For medium size only: Knit 2 rnds in mc.		
SHAPING THE TOE		
Round 1: *K1 with cc B, K1 with cc C; repeat from * to end of rnd.		
Round 2: *K1 with cc C, K1 with cc B; repeat from * to end of rnd.		

Round 3
   Needle 1: With mc, K1, ssk, knit to last 3 sts, K2tog, K1.
 	
   Needle 2: K1, ssk, knit to end.
 	
   Needle 3: Knit to last 3 sts, K2tog, K1.		

Next Rounds: Repeat Round 1 until you have 5 sts on Needle 1, 3 sts on Needle 2, and 2 sts on Needle 3.		
Slip the sts from Needle 2 to Needle 3 and graft the toe with Kitchener Stitch (see illustrations and instructions on page 89).		
Cut the yarn and weave in loose ends.		

Kitchener Stitch

1. Hold two fabric layers together with purl sides facing. Using a needle, draw yarn through first stitch of front needle as if to knit; slip stitch off.

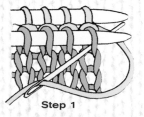

Step 1

2. Draw yarn through second stitch of front needle as if to purl; leave stitch on needle.

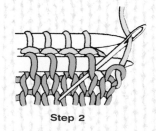

Step 2

3. Draw yarn through first stitch of back needle as if to purl; slip stitch off.

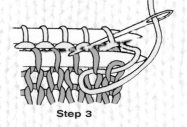

Step 3

4. Draw yarn through second stitch of back needle as if to knit; leave stitch on. Repeat Steps 1–4 until no stitches remain on needles.

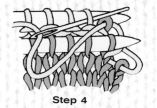

Step 4

MAKING THE LADYBUG DANGLES	INFANT S	INFANT M
NOTE: Instructions are for one dangle. Make four dangles, two for each sock. Refer to the Ladybug Dangle Chart on page 91, starting at the bottom, with Line 1, and working from right to left.		
With #3 (3.25mm) needles, use cc C and loosely cast on 3 sts. So that rows and chart lines correspond, we are referring to the cast-on as Row 1.		

	INFANT S	INFANT M
Row 2 (purl row; Line 2): Inc 2 in all 3 sts. You will have	9 sts	9 sts
Row 3: K1, inc 1 in the next 3 sts, K1, inc 1 in the next 3 sts, K1. You will have	15 sts	15 sts
Rows 4–9: Knit the 15 sts, following Ladybug Dangle Chart on page 91.		
Row 10: P1, P2tog 3 times, P1, P2tog 3 times, P1. You will have	9 sts	9 sts
Row 11: K2tog twice, K1, K2tog twice. You will have	5 sts	5 sts
Cut the yarn and pull it through the remaining sts. Sew the seam with the wrong sides together, leaving a hole for stuffing. Stuff the ladybug lightly and sew up the hole.		
MAKING THE LACES		
Insert the crochet hook into the nose (top) of one ladybug dangle and, using mc, make 50 chains (see page 91 for instructions on making chain sts). Cut the yarn, leaving a generous tail, and pull it through the last chain. Starting at the hole at the right side of the right sock and the left side of the left sock, weave the chain through all the eyelets. Attach the second ladybug dangle securely to the other end of the chain.		

**LADYBUG BAND CHART
SMALL SIZE**

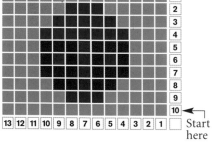

Start here

**LADYBUG BAND CHART
MEDIUM SIZE**

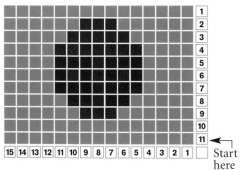

Start here

 = cc A

■ = cc B

■ = cc C

LADYBUG DANGLE CHART

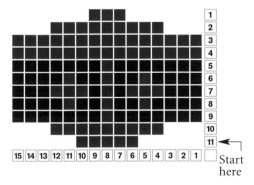

15 14 13 12 11 10 9 8 7 6 5 4 3 2 1 □ Start here

1
2
3
4
5
6
7
8
9
10
11 ◄—

Chain Stitch

With one loop on your crochet hook, insert the hook under the working yarn from right to left. Twist the hook counterclockwise to catch a loop of yarn, and draw it through the loop already on the hook.

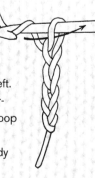

Lettuce-Edge Booties

Designed by Linda Daniels, Northampton Wools

These booties are knitted flat, rather than in the round, and are folded over and sewn together at the end. The lettuce edge, which is made by casting on four times as many stitches as you need and decreasing rapidly, lends a frilly touch to the ribbed cuff. The foot is worked in garter stitch, where every row is knitted — nothing could be simpler!

Sizes and approximate lengths:
Infant small (0–3 months), 3" (7.5cm)
Infant large (3–12 months), 4" (10cm)
Yarn: Filatura di Crosa 501, 100% superwash merino wool, double-knit weight
Small:
   50 yds (45m) mc (raspberry/#2120 or yellow/#503)
   5 yds (4m) cc (multi/#9501 or multi/#9503)
Large:
   65 yds (59m) mc (raspberry/#2120 or yellow/#503)
   5 yds (4m) cc (multi/#9501 or multi/#9503)
Needles: Three #5 (3.75mm) straight needles
Tip: Place needle tip protectors on one end of dp needles to create easy-to-maneuver "straight needles."
Gauge: 20 sts = 4" (10cm) on #5 (3.75mm) needles in garter st
Other supplies: Stitch holders or safety pins; yarn needle

---

cc = contrasting color ◆ **K** = knit ◆ **K2tog** = knit 2 stitches together ◆ **mc** = main color
P = purl ◆ **P2tog** = purl 2 stitches together ◆ **sl** = slip ◆ **st(s)** = stitch(es) ◆ **yd(s)** = yard(s)

KNITTING THE CUFF	INFANT S	INFANT L
NOTE: The instructions given are for one bootie. Left and right booties are identical.		
With #5 (3.75mm) needles and cc, cast on	80 sts	120 sts
Row 1: *K2, pass first st over second st; repeat from * to end of row. You will have	40 sts	60 sts
Row 2: P2tog across row. You will have	20 sts	30 sts
Row 3: Change to mc and knit to end of row.		
Row 4: Purl to end of row.		
Rows 5–14: Work in K1, P1 ribbing.		
DIVIDING FOR INSTEP		
Row 1: Knit	14 sts	21 sts
Place on a stitch holder the remaining	6 sts	9 sts
Row 2: Turn, and knit	8 sts	12 sts
Place on a stitch holder the remaining	6 sts	9 sts
Row 3: Turn and knit to end of row.		
Next Rows: Repeat Row 3 until you have completed	14 rows (7 ridges)	16 rows (8 ridges)
KNITTING THE FOOT		
Row 1 (right side): Knit	8 sts	12 sts
Pick up and K8 along left side of instep (the side of the rows you just knitted.)		
Slide the stitches from the next stitch holder onto the empty needle and knit them. You will have	22 sts	29 sts

	INFANT S	INFANT L
Row 2: Knit to end of needle, then pick up and P8 along right side of instep. Slip the stitches from the remaining stitch holder onto the empty needle and knit them. You will have	36 sts	46 sts
DECREASING FOR THE TOES		
Row 1: K(A), K2tog, K(B), K2tog, K(A).	A = 12 sts, B = 8 sts	A = 15 sts, B = 12 sts
You will have	34 sts	44 sts
Row 2: Knit to end of row.		
Row 3: K(A), K2tog, K(B), K2tog, K(A).	A = 11 sts, B = 8 sts	A = 14 sts, B = 12 sts
You will have	32 sts	42 sts
Row 4: Knit to end of row.		
Row 5: K(A), K2tog, K(B), K2tog, K(A).	A = 10 sts, B = 8 sts	A = 13 sts, B = 12 sts
You will have	30 sts	40 sts
Rows 6–10: Knit to end of each row.		
FINISHING THE BOOTIE		
Knit	15 sts	20 sts
Use the three-needle cast-off technique (see instructions on page 13) to knit the bootie together at the toe.		
Using a yarn needle, sew the back seam and weave in the ends.		

Puppy Slippers

Designed by Beverly Galeskas, Fiber Trends

With their floppy ears and red tongues, these slippers roll over and beg for your attention. The ears, tongues, and tails are knitted separately and sewn onto the slippers, then the slippers are felted so they will keep their shape and be warm and weatherproof. The cuffs, eyes, and noses are added after felting.

cc = contrasting color ◆ **dp** = double point ◆ **K** = knit ◆ **K2tog** = knit 2 stitches together ◆ **K3tog** = knit 3 stitches together ◆ **M1** = make 1 **mc** = main color ◆ **P** = purl ◆ **psso** = pass slip stitch over ◆ **rnd(s)** = round(s) **sl** = slip ◆ **ssk** = slip, slip, knit the 2 slipped stitches together ◆ **st(s)** = stitch(es) ◆ **St st** = stockinette stitch **W&T** = wrap and turn

Sizes and approximate finished lengths:
Infant small (0–3 months), 3¾" (9.4cm)
Infant medium (3–6 months), 4" (10cm)
Infant large (6–9 months), 4¼" (10.6cm)
NOTE: Exact finished lengths will be determined by the yarn and the point at which you stop felting.
Yarn: Bryspun kid-n-ewe, 50% wool/50% kid mohair, worsted weight
Small: 70 yds (63m) mc (brown), 1 yds (1m) cc A (red), 35 yds (32m) cc B (black)
Medium: 85 yds (77m) mc (brown), 20 yds (18m) cc A (red), 40 yds (36m) cc B (black)
Large: 95 yds (86m) mc (brown), 1 yd (1m) cc A (red), 45 yds (41m) cc B (black)
NOTE: For information on other yarns suitable for felting, see Felting Tips on page 45. Cc B, which is used for the cuff that is added after the slippers have been felted, can be any worsted weight yarn.

Needles
One set #5 (3.75mm) dp needles
One set #8 (5.0mm) straight needles
One set #10 (6.0mm) straight needles
Gauge: 15 sts = 4" (10cm) on #10 (6.0mm) needles in St st, before felting
Other supplies: 10 yds (9m) of smooth, colorfast waste cotton in about the same thickness as the main yarn; small amount of black embroidery floss for eyes; two ready-made black pompoms for noses, each ½" (1.25cm); yarn needle; embroidery needle

KNITTING THE SLIPPERS	INFANT S	INFANT M	INFANT L
NOTE: The instructions given are for one slipper. Left and right slippers are identical.			
With #10 (6.0mm) needles and mc, cast on	31 sts	35 sts	39 sts
Row 1: Knit to end of row.			
Row 2: *K1, M1, K (see column at right), M1; repeat from *, then K1.	14 sts	16 sts	18 sts
You will have	35 sts	39 sts	43 sts
Row 3: K (see column at right), W&T. **NOTE:** See How to Wrap and Turn (W&T) on page 27.	26 sts	29 sts	32 sts
K (see column at right), M1, K1, M1, K (see column at right), W&T, knit to end of row.	8 sts	9 sts	10 sts
You will have	37 sts	41 sts	45 sts
Row 4: K1, M1, K (see column at right), M1, K3, M1, K (see column at right), M1, K1.	16 sts	18 sts	20 sts
You will have	41 sts	45 sts	49 sts
Row 5: Knit to end of row.			
Row 6: K1, M1, K (see column at right), M1, K5, M1, K (see column at right), M1, K1.	17 sts	19 sts	21 sts
You will have	45 sts	49 sts	53 sts
Rows 7–11: Knit to end of each row.			
Row 12: K(A), ssk, K(B), K2tog, K(A).	A=17 sts, B=7 sts	A=18 sts, B=9 sts	A=20 sts, B=9 sts

	INFANT S	INFANT M	INFANT L
You will have	43 sts	47 sts	51 sts
Rows 13, 15, 17, 19, 21, 23, and 25: Knit to end of each row.			
Row 14: K(A), ssk, K(B), K2tog, K(A).	A = 17 sts, B = 5 sts	A = 18 sts, B = 7 sts	A = 20 sts, B = 7 sts
You will have	41 sts	45 sts	49 sts
Row 16: K(A), ssk, K(B), K2tog, K(A).	A = 17 sts, B = 3 sts	A = 18 sts, B = 5 sts	A = 20 sts, B = 5 sts
You will have	39 sts	43 sts	47 sts
Row 18: K(A), ssk, K(B), K2tog, K(A).	A = 17 sts, B = 1 st	A = 18 sts, B = 3 sts	A = 20 sts, B = 3 sts
You will have	37 sts	41 sts	45 sts
Row 20: K (see column at right), ssk, K1, K2tog, K (see column at right).	16 sts	18 sts	20 sts
You will have	35 sts	39 sts	43 sts
Row 22: K (see column at right), ssk, K1, K2tog, K (see column at right).	15 sts	17 sts	19 sts
You will have	33 sts	37 sts	41 sts
Row 24: K (see column at right), ssk, K1, K2tog, K (see column at right).	14 sts	16 sts	18 sts
You will have	31 sts	35 sts	39 sts
For small size only: Cast off all stitches knitwise after Row 24. Cut the yarn and fasten off.			

	INFANT S	INFANT M	INFANT L
Row 26, *for medium and large sizes only:* K (see column at right), ssk, K1, K2tog, K (see column at right).		15 sts	17 sts
You will have		33 sts	37 sts
Cast off all stitches knitwise. Cut the yarn and fasten off.			
KNITTING THE EARS			
NOTE: The instructions given are for one ear. Make four identical ears.			
With #8 (5.0mm) needles and mc, cast on	5 sts	5 sts	5 sts
Rows 1 and 2: Knit to end of each row.			
Row 3: K2, M1, K1, M1, K2. You will have	7 sts	7 sts	7 sts
Rows 4–10: Knit to end of each row.			
Row 11: K1, ssk, K1, K2tog, K1. You will have	5 sts	5 sts	5 sts
Rows 12–14: Knit to end of each row.			
Row 15: Ssk, K1, K2tog. You will have	3 sts	3 sts	3 sts
Row 16: K3tog. Cut the yarn and fasten off.			
KNITTING THE TONGUES			
NOTE: The instructions given are for one tongue. Make two identical tongues.			
With #8 (5.0mm) needles and cc A, cast on	3 sts	3 sts	3 sts

	INFANT S	INFANT M	INFANT L
Rows 1 and 2: Knit to end of each row.			
Row 3: Sl 1, K2tog, psso. Cut the yarn and fasten off.			
KNITTING THE TAILS			
NOTE: The instructions given are for one tail. Make two identical tails.			
With #8 (5.0mm) needles and mc, cast on	2 sts	2 sts	2 sts
Make a 2"-long I-cord (see I-Cords on page 23). Cut the yarn, leaving an 8" tail.			
With a yarn needle, thread the yarn through the sts to fasten it, then run it down through the center of the cord. Pull lightly to give a slight bend to the tail, then fasten off.			
ASSEMBLING THE SLIPPERS			
The cast-off edge is the top where the cuff will be. Pin the ears to the third ridge down from the top, close to the center, pointing downward. Adjust their positions until you are satisfied with the appearance.			
With a yarn needle and mc, sew the ears into place across the base of each ear, using a backstitch.			
Count down from the top (see column at right) then pin the tongue centered on the work, and attach it in the same way as the ears.	9 ridges	10 ridges	10 ridges
With a yarn needle and mc, sew the center back and bottom seams, keeping the seams flat and sewing only the edges.			
With a yarn needle and mc, sew the tails to the backs of the slippers.			

	INFANT S	INFANT M	INFANT L
Work in all the yarn ends.			
With waste cotton and three dp needles, pick up, evenly spaced around the top of the slipper,	24 sts	26 sts	28 sts
Divide the stitches evenly among the three needles. **NOTE:** For advice about knitting in the round on dp needles, see Round Robin on pages 17–18.			
Knit 3 rnds, then cast off.			
FELTING THE SLIPPERS			
Felt the slippers, following the Felting Instructions on page 20. While the slippers are drying, shape the ears and curl the tails.			
KNITTING THE CUFFS			
With dp needles and cc B, pick up stitches at the base of the waste-cotton sts through the felt along the upper edge of the slippers. You will have	24 sts	26 sts	28 sts
Cut the waste cotton and remove it.			
Distribute the sts evenly among three dp needles and work in K1, P1 ribbing for about 3". Cast off loosely while working the last rnd.			
MAKING THE FACES			
To make the puppy's eyes, loop embroidery thread several times around a sharp needle, then insert the needle into the slipper and knot it on the wrong side (French knot).			
Sew on pompoms for the noses, or make your own, following the instructions in Pompoms on page 22.			

PUPPY SLIPPERS

Felted Slipper Socks

Designed by Cindy Walker, Stony Hill Fiberarts

While these may look like shoes and socks, they're really one-piece slippers. The "shoe," made from a mohair/wool blend, is felted to keep it warm and snug. The sole is made first, then the sides of the shoe; the sock, which is made of stretchy cotton or any yarn that doesn't felt, is knitted onto the shoe, and the ribbed cuff is worked last.

Sizes and approximate finished lengths:

Small (3–12 months), 4" (10cm)

Medium (12–18 months), 5" (12.5cm)

Large (18–30 months), 6" (15cm)

NOTE: Exact finished lengths will be determined by the yarn and the point at which you stop felting.

Yarn: Henry's Attic "Texas" and "Pony" double-skeined together, 55% mohair/45% wool, hand-dyed by the designer, or other natural animal fiber in worsted or double-knit weight (For other suitable yarns, see page 41.)

Small: 60 yds (54m) mc (blue)

Medium: 70 yds (63m) mc (blue)

Large: 100 yds (90m) mc (blue)

Elasticized cotton: Cascade Fixation

Small: 26 yds (23m) cc (white)

Medium: 41 yds (37m) cc (white)

Large: 58 yds (52m) cc (white)

Needles

One set #3 (3.25mm) dp needles

One #10½ (6.5mm) circular needle, 16" (40.5cm) long

Gauge

Wool: 13 sts = 4" (10cm) on #10½ (6.5mm) needles in St st, before felting

Cotton: 28 sts = 4" (10cm) on #3 (3.25mm) needles in St st

Other supplies: Yarn needle, stitch markers, stitch holder, suede or leather for sole, nylon thread for attaching sole

---

cc = contrasting color ◆ **dp** = double point ◆ **inc** = increase ◆ **K** = knit **K2tog** = knit 2 stitches together **mc** = main color ◆ **P** = purl ◆ **P2tog** = purl 2 stitches together ◆ **psso** = pass slip stitch over ◆ **rnd(s)** = round(s) ◆ **sl** = slip **st(s)** = stitch(es) ◆ **St st** = stockinette stitch ◆ **yd(s)** = yard(s)

KNITTING THE SOLES	SMALL	MEDIUM	LARGE
NOTE: The instructions given are for one sole. Left and right soles are identical. See the illustration on page 55. The sole is knit in rows, back and forth on a circular needle. Do not join cast-on into a round.			
With the #10½ (6.5mm) circular needle and mc, using the long-tail method, cast on	3 sts	6 sts	7 sts
Row 1 and all odd-numbered rows: Knit to end of each row.			
Row 2 (right side): K1, inc 1,	inc 1	K4	K3, inc 1, K1
You will have	5 sts	7 sts	9 sts
Row 4: K1, inc 1, knit to last 2 sts, inc 1, K1. You will have	7 sts	9 sts	11 sts
Row 6: K1, inc 1, knit to last 2 sts, inc 1, K1. You will have	9 sts	11 sts	13 sts
Row 8: K1, inc 1, knit to last 2 sts, inc 1, K1. You will have	11 sts	13 sts	15 sts
Row 10: K1, inc 1, knit to last 2 sts, inc 1, K1. You will have	13 sts	15 sts	17 sts
For medium and large sizes only, Row 12: K1, inc 1, knit to last 2 sts, inc 1, K1. You will have		17 sts	19 sts
For all sizes: Continue knitting in garter st to the end of	Row 29	Row 35	Row 41
On the right side of the work, you will have	15 ridges	18 ridges	21 ridges
First decrease row: K1, K2tog, knit to last 3 sts, K2tog, K1. You will have	11 sts	15 sts	17 sts
Continue knitting in garter st to the end of	Row 35	Row 41	Row 53

	SMALL	MEDIUM	LARGE
On the right side of the work, you will have	18 ridges	21 ridges	27 ridges
Second decrease row: K1, K2tog, knit to last 3 sts, K2tog, K1. You will have	9 sts	13 sts	15 sts
Continue knitting in garter st, decreasing 2 sts every other row until 3 sts remain. On the right side of work, you will have	22 ridges	27 ridges	33 ridges
Last row: Sl 1 knitwise, K2tog, psso. Leave the final st loose.			
KNITTING THE SIDES			
Keeping the final st on the needle and with right side facing you, go around the outer edge of the sole, picking up additional sts by slipping the outermost loop of each ridge onto the #10½ (6.5mm) circular needle. Make sure sts are evenly spaced so the slipper will not be lopsided. In addition to the stitch remaining on the needle, pick up	44 sts	56 sts	68 sts
Mark the first st (back of heel). Place a marker between the two stitches at the front of the toe.			
NOTE: For advice about knitting in the round on a circular needle, see Round Robin on pages 17–18.			
Rounds 1, 3, 5, and 7: Purl to end of rnd.			
Round 2: Knit to end of rnd.			
Round 4 *For small size:* K17, (K2tog, K1) 2 more times, K2tog, K17. You will have *For medium size:* K21, (K2tog, K1, K2tog) 2 more times, K21. You will have *For large size:* K26, (K2tog, K1) 4 more times, K2tog, K26. You will have	41 sts	51 sts	63 sts

	SMALL	MEDIUM	LARGE
Round 6 *For small size:* K17, K2tog, K3, K2tog, K17. You will have	39 sts		
For medium size: K21, K2tog twice, K1, K2tog twice, K21. You will have		47 sts	
For large size: K26, (K2tog, K1) 3 times, K2tog, K26. You will have			59 sts
Cut the wool yarn, leaving a tail to weave in before felting. Sl the first (see column at right) onto the right-hand needle.	18 sts	21 sts	27 sts
MAKING THE TOP OF THE FOOT			
NOTE: For this section you will turn the work with every row instead of knitting in the round.			
Row 1: With the first dp needle and the elasticized cotton (cc), knit the next	3 sts	5 sts	5 sts
Row 2: With the second dp needle, P (see column at right), then P1 from the slipped sts on the circular needle.	3 sts	5 sts	5 sts
Row 3: K (see column at right), K1 from circular needle.	4 sts	6 sts	6 sts
You will have	5 sts	7 sts	7 sts
Repeat Rows 2 and 3, ending with a purl row when the dp needle has	10 sts	12 sts	16 sts
The circular needle has	29 sts	35 sts	43 sts
Next row: Knit to last 2 sts, K2tog, K1 from circular needle.			

	SMALL	MEDIUM	LARGE
Next row: Purl to last 2 sts, P2tog, P1 from circular needle. **NOTE:** Use the Twisted Purl Decrease method, below, to P2tog.			
Repeat these two rows until the circular needle has	17 sts	21 sts	27 sts
The dp needle still has	10 sts	12 sts	16 sts
Last row: Knit to last 2 sts, K2tog. The dp needle now has	9 sts	11 sts	15 sts
KNITTING THE SOCK CUFF			
NOTE: See illustration below.			
Leaving the sts on the dp needle, take a second dp needle and knit from the circular needle	9 sts	11 sts	14 sts
With the third dp needle, knit from the circular needle	8 sts	10 sts	13 sts

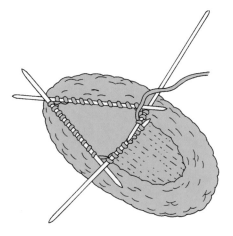

Knitting the sock cuff

Twisted Purl Decrease

This way of purling 2 stitches together results in a neat finish on the right side of the work. Use it for the slipper tops for a more balanced effect.

1. Slip 2 stitches knitwise, then slide them back onto the left needle.
2. Purl the 2 stitches together through the back, bringing the right needle behind the 2 stitches. Come up through the bottom of the two loops, so that your working needle comes in front of the other.

	SMALL	MEDIUM	LARGE
There should be no sts left on the circular needle. The dp needles have a total of	26 sts	32 sts	42 sts
You will now start knitting in the round, beginning with the needle across the front of the slipper.			
Rounds 1–4: Knit even to the end of each rnd.			
Round 5: Change to K1, P1 ribbing and work for 1.5" (4cm) or more, if desired.			
Cast off loosely and sew in all the loose ends.			
TIP: To cast off loosely, knit the first stitch as usual. Knit the second stitch, but don't slide it off the left needle. Bring the left needle to the front and pull the first stitch over the second, then slide off the left stitch. Repeat with remaining stitches. This forces you to keep the bound-off stitches loose.			
FELTING			
Felt the slippers, following the Felting Instructions on page 20.			
FINISHING UP			
To keep toddlers from slipping, you may want to sew on a suede or leather sole (see photo on page 63). Place the dried and shaped slipper on a scrap of suede and draw around the edge. Cut out the suede sole and sew it to the slipper with nylon thread.			

Little Speckled Toes

Designed by Lynda Gemmell, Cabin Fever

Colorful, textured yarn lends these ankle socks an insouciant touch of style, though you could make them out of any washable double-knit weight yarn. What better way to use up leftover ends of yarn? The socks are fast and straightforward to knit, and warm and cozy for little feet. It's best to use short needles (5"/13cm, ideally) when you're knitting tiny socks in the round.

Sizes and approximate finished lengths:
Infant, 4" (10cm)
1 year, 4½" (11.5cm)
2 years, 5" (12.5cm)
Yarn: Naturally Magic Garden Buttons, 83% wool/17% polyester, machine washable, double-knit weight
Infant: 50 yds (45m) mc (denim, mango, purple, turquoise, or hot pink)
1 year: 65 yds (59m) mc (denim, mango, purple, turquoise, or hot pink)
2 years: 75 yds (68m) mc (denim, mango, purple, turquoise, or hot pink)
Needles: Five #3 (3.25mm) dp needles, 5 inches long
Gauge: 24 sts = 4" (10cm) on #3 (3.25mm) needles in St st
Other supplies: Yarn needle

dp = double point ◆ **K** = knit ◆ **K2tog** = knit 2 stitches together ◆ **P** = purl ◆ **P2tog** = purl 2 stitches together ◆ **rnd(s)** = round(s) ◆ **sl** = slip ◆ **ssk** = slip, slip, knit 2 slipped together ◆ **st(s)** = stitch(es) ◆ **St st** = stockinette stitch ◆ **yd(s)** = yard(s)

KNITTING THE CUFF	INFANT	1 YEAR	2 YEARS
NOTE: The instructions given are for one sock. Left and right socks are identical.			
For advice about knitting in the round with double point needles, see Round Robin on page 17–18.			
With #3 (3.25mm) needles and mc, loosely cast on	36 sts	36 sts	36 sts
Divide the sts evenly among four needles.			
Work in K1, P1 ribbing until the piece measures	3" (7.5cm)	3¼" (8cm)	3½" (9cm)
Work in St st for	4 rnds	5 rnds	6 rnds
KNITTING THE HEEL FLAP			
K9 sts across Needle 1, then turn work, and on a single needle sl 1, P17 sts. You now have one needle with 18 sts for the heel flap. Divide the remaining 18 sts evenly on the other two needles for the instep.			

Using only the 18 sts for the heel flap, work back and forth on two needles, turning at the end of each row, as follows:
 	
    Odd-numbered rows (right side of work): Sl 1, knit to end of row.
 	
    Even-numbered rows (wrong side of work): Sl 1, purl to end of row.			

Stop at the end of a purl row when the measurement from the end of the ribbing is	1¼" (3cm)	1¾" (4.5cm)	2¼" (5.5cm)
TURNING THE HEEL			
Continue to work the 18 heel sts on two needles.			

	INFANT	1 YEAR	2 YEARS
Row 1: K13, ssk, turn.			
Row 2: Sl 1, P8, P2tog, turn.			
Row 3: Sl 1, K8, ssk, turn.			
Row 4: Sl 1, P8, P2tog, turn.			
Rows 5–8: Repeat Rows 3 and 4 until all side sts have been worked and you have 10 sts on the needle, ending with a purl row.			
K5 to middle of a right-side row.			
KNITTING THE INSTEP			
You are now back to knitting in the round with five needles. Each round begins at the center back of the heel.			
Round 1: Using a new needle, K5, then pick up and K (see column at right) along the right side of the heel.	7 sts	8 sts	9 sts
Knit the 18 instep sts, keeping them on their two needles.			
With the last needle, pick up and K (see column at right) along the left side of the heel and work across the last 5 heel sts.	7 sts	8 sts	9 sts
Needles 1 and 4 each have	12 sts	13 sts	14 sts
Needles 2 and 3 each have	9 sts	9 sts	9 sts
All needles have a total of	42 sts	44 sts	46 sts

	INFANT	1 YEAR	2 YEARS
Round 2 Needle 1: (See column at right), K2tog, K1. Needles 2 and 3: Knit to end of needle. Needle 4: K1, ssk,	K9	K10	K11
Round 3 and all odd-numbered rounds: Knit to end of rnd.			
Round 4 Needle 1: K (see column at right), K2tog, K1. Needles 2 and 3: Knit to end of needle. Needle 4: K1, ssk,	8 sts	9 sts	10 sts
You now have	38 sts	40 sts	42 sts
Continue in the same way, decreasing 1st in each even-numbered rnd at the end of Needle 1 and the beginning of Needle 4, until you have a total of 36 sts, with 9 sts on each of four needles.			
Knit the 36 sts until measurement from the end of the heel flap (before turning the heel) is	1" (2.5cm)	2½" (6.5cm)	3" (7.5cm)
SHAPING THE TOE			
Round 1 Needle 1: K6, K2tog, K1. Needle 2: K1, ssk, K6. Needle 3: K6, K2tog, K1. Needle 4: K1, ssk, K6.			
You now have 32 sts, with 8 sts on each needle.			
Round 2: Knit.			

	INFANT	1 YEAR	2 YEARS
Continue in the same way, decreasing 4 sts in each odd-numbered rnd until you have a total of 20 sts, with 5 sts on each of four needles, then decrease 4 sts every rnd until you have 8 sts, with 2 sts on each needle.			
Using a yarn needle, pass the yarn through all the remaining sts, pull tight, and sew in the ends.			

Jive with Five

Many knitters learned to knit socks and other tubular projects using a set of four double point needles. This pattern suggests using five. If you're accustomed to knitting with only four, you'll quickly see that using five has several advantages, especially for such a relatively small diameter project. The first thing you'll notice is that it's more comfortable, since the fabric relaxes more easily into a square than it would into a triangle. The end result is better as well. Because there's less stretching around those corners where the needles meet, you'll find that the corner stitches are less likely to stretch and leave that tell-tale line. Try five and come alive!

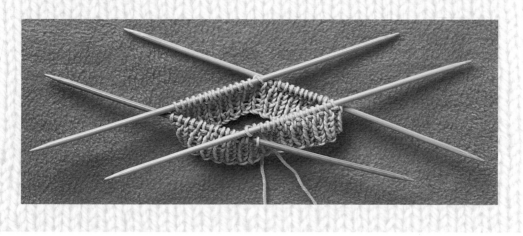

Striped Stocking Cap

Designed by Deb Gemmell, Cabin Fever

This simple stocking cap offers endless possibilities. Pastel stripes are soft and beautiful for spring; red and white stripes are classic for the holiday season. And who says you can use only two colors? If you're trying to finish up odds and ends of yarn, make each stripe a different color. The long, knotted I-cord at the top and the rolled-up brim are elegant details that complement any color choice.

Sizes and circumferences:
Small (3–6 months), 17" (43cm)
Medium (1 year), 18" (45.5cm)
Yarn: Butterfly Super 10, 100% cotton, double-knit weight
Small: 90 yds (81m) mc (white), 60 yds (54m) cc (lilac)
Medium: 110 yds (99m) mc (white), 75 yds (68m) cc (lilac)
Needles
One set #6 (4.0mm) dp needles
One #6 (4.0mm) circular needle, 16" (40cm) long
Gauge: 22 sts = 4" (10cm) on #6 (4.0mm) needles in St st
Other supplies: Yarn needle; stitch marker

---

cc = contrasting color ◆ **dp** = double point ◆ **K** = knit ◆ **M1** = make 1 ◆ **mc** = main color **rnd(s)** = round(s) ◆ **st(s)** = stitch(es) ◆ **St st** = stockinette stitch ◆ **yd(s)** = yard(s)

MAKING THE I-CORD	SMALL	MEDIUM
With dp needles and mc, cast on 5 sts. Using two needles, make a 5" (12.5cm) I-cord and tie a knot in it. For instructions, see I-Cords on page 23.		
After the last rnd, redistribute the sts onto two dp needles so you can knit with the third needle. **NOTE:** For advice about knitting in the round with double point and circular needles, see Round Robin on pages 17–18.		
Round 1: With mc, *K1, M1; repeat from * to end of rnd. You will have (see column at right). Put a stitch marker through the first st of the rnd.	10 sts	10 sts
Rounds 2–6: With mc, knit even in St st. Cut the yarn now and each time you switch colors, rather than carrying it to the next stripe. Leave a 3" tail, and refer to Hiding Color Jogs, page 121.		
Stripe #1 (cc) Rounds 7–10: Change to cc and knit even in St st. Round 11: *K1, M1; repeat from * to end of rnd. You will have	20 sts	20 sts
Redistribute your sts among three needles so you can knit with the fourth needle. Change to the circular needle when you have enough stitches.		
Stripe #2 (mc) Rounds 12–16: Change to mc and knit even in St st.		
Stripe #3 (cc) Rounds 17–20: Change to cc and knit even in St st. Round 21: *K2, M1; repeat from * to end of rnd. You will have	30 sts	30 sts

MAKING MORE STRIPES	SMALL	MEDIUM
Continue in the stripe pattern, working even in St st for 5 rnds of mc and 4 rnds of cc, then increasing 10 sts in the fifth cc rnd until you have	90 sts	100 sts
Work in St st in alternating bands of mc and cc without any increases for an additional	3" (7.5cm)	3" (7.5cm)
KNITTING THE BRIM		
With mc, knit an additional 2" (5cm) for the rolled edge. Cast off loosely.		
FINISHING UP		
Sew in the ends. The end of the cast-off round should be sewn on the right side so it won't show when the brim is rolled up. Sew in tails as described below.		

Hiding Color Jogs

To make a smooth transition from one color to the next, sew in the loose ends on the diagonal, as shown. The tails from the beginnings of the stripes are sewn up and to the left, while the tails from the ends of the stripes are sewn down and to the right. This trick gets rid of the "jog" where a new color starts.

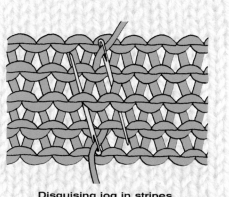

Disguising jog in stripes

Contributing Designers

Northampton Wools
11 Pleasant Street
Northampton, MA 01060
(413) 586-4331
e-mail: NohoKnit@aol.com

Since 1988, **Linda Daniels** has owned and operated Northampton Wools, a full-service retail store offering knitting classes and a wide selection of yarns from around the world. *Interweave Knits* has featured many of her patterns, and she designed and knit actor Michael Caine's vest and several sweaters for the movie *The Cider House Rules.*

Fiber Trends
P.O. Box 7266
East Wenatchee, WA 98802
(509) 884-8631
www.fibertrends.com

Beverly Galeskas is the owner and founder of Fiber Trends Pattern Company. Along with other designing, Bev is always looking for new ways to use the fascinating technique of knitting and felting (fulling) to create unique garments, accessories, and toys. She has taught classes at TNNA, Stitches, and many other knitting and fiber shows. Fiber Trends patterns are available at yarn stores across North America. An extensive listing of stores can be found on her Web site; in an effort to support those stores, she does not offer direct mail order. "I believe my experiences of learning to knit as an adult and then teaching beginning knitting in my yarn store were the best training for writing patterns for others," she says.

Cabin Fever
111 Nottawasaga Street
Orillia, ON L3V 3J7
Canada
(800) 671-9112
www.cabinfever.ca

Canadian sisters **Deb and Lynda Gemmell** own and operate Cabin Fever, a hand-knitting pattern publisher. The innovative duo design dozens of patterns for sweaters, hats, socks, and other apparel that are sold in yarn shops across North America. Most are knit in the round and in one piece, with virtually no sewing required. Plus sizes are also a standard element of most of their patterns.

Nancy Lindberg
69 East Golden Lake Road
Circle Pines, MN 55014
e-mail: Nlpatterns@prodigy.net

Nancy Lindberg developed her teaching skills while owning a yarn shop in Minneapolis for more than a decade. She moved on to pattern designing and continues to teach, an activity that has garnered a large and faithful following. Her patterns appeal to all knitting levels and are available in yarn shops across the United States.

Woodsmoke Woolworks
1335 Route 102
Upper Gagetown, NB E5M 1R5
Canada
(506) 488-2044
e-mail: woodsmke@nbnet.nb.ca

Barbara Telford doesn't remember not knowing how to knit. A member of the Canadian Knitwear Designers Association and a juried member of the New Brunswick Craft Council, she runs Woodsmoke Woolworks, a farm-based knitwear and design shop. She won the New Brunswick Craft Council's Oudemans Christmas Choice Award in 2002 for the ingenuity of her knitted hat collection. Her unique work is outstanding for its originality and her ability to manipulate wool to produce witty and lively designs. "I don't know where the designs came from," she says, "but I am glad they came."

Stony Hill Fiberarts
3525 Durham Road
Raleigh, NC 27614
(888) 849-9440
www.stonyhillfiberarts.com

Cindy Walker established Stony Hill Fiberarts in 1994. Her company produces felted baby hats, baby booties, and slippers; felted knitting patterns that are simply written; hand-dyed yarn to ensure reliable felting results; and whimsical, handcrafted knitting needles. Cindy also contributed some of her delightfully upbeat and loving insights into knitting for babies to the introduction to this book. As she says, "Knitting has been my saving grace. I firmly believe that when we engage ourselves in some type of art, we expand our life experience in such a positive way that all we come in contact with is enriched: ourselves, our families, our world. I am grateful to have discovered this truth. And . . . it's cheaper than therapy!"

Acknowledgments

Many thanks to

The knitters and test knitters who helped make the projects for this book:
Marjorie Anderson, Pamela Art, Kathleen Case, Linda Daniels, Beverly Galeskas,
Deb Gemmell, Lynda Gemmell, Mary Johnson, Karen Levy, Nancy Lindberg, Tina Murphy,
Rita Riley, Martha Storey, Barbara Telford, Carolynn Vincent, and Cindy Walker.

The companies that supplied yarn:
Brown Sheep Company of Mitchell, Nebraska
Tahki Stacy Charles of Brooklyn, New York

The yarn stores that offered invaluable advice:
The Naked Sheep, Bennington, Vermont
Northampton Wools, Northampton, Massachusetts
WEBS, Northampton, Massachusetts
Woolcott & Co., Cambridge, Massachusetts

Index

Page numbers in *italics* indicate photos or illustrations.
Page numbers in **bold** indicate tables or charts.

Other Storey Titles You Will Enjoy

Knit Baby Blankets! edited by Gwen Steege
Hardcover
ISBN 1-58017-495-7
Full-color photographs and
illustrations throughout
128 pages

Knit Hats! edited by Gwen Steege
Hardcover
ISBN 1-58017-482-5
Full-color photographs and
illustrations throughout
96 pages

Knit Mittens! by Robin Hansen
Hardcover
ISBN 1-58017-483-3
Full-color photographs and
illustrations throughout
128 pages

Knit Christmas Stockings! edited by Gwen Steege
Hardcover
ISBN 1-58017-505-8
Full-color photographs and
illustrations throughout
136 pages

Available wherever books are sold.